THE MUSIC BOOK

Eunice Boardman
Professor of Music Education
University of Wisconsin
Madison, Wisconsin

Barbara Andress
Professor of Music Education
Arizona State University
Tempe, Arizona

Special Consultants

Beth Landis
Former Director of Music Education
City Schools
Riverside, California

Betty Welsbacher
Director of Special Music Education
Wichita State University
Wichita, Kansas

Consultants

Martha Mahoney
Elementary Music Department Head
Elementary Schools
Milford, Connecticut

Donald Regier
Supervisor of Vocal Music
Secondary Schools
Baltimore County, Maryland

Keith Thompson
Associate Professor, Music Education
Pennsylvania State University
University Park, Pennsylvania

Nelmatilda Woodard
Director, Bureau of Music Education
Board of Education
City of Chicago

Holt, Rinehart and Winston, Publishers
New York, Toronto, London, Sydney

Copyright © 1981 by Holt, Rinehart and Winston, Publishers
All rights reserved
Printed in the United States of America
ISBN: 0-03-042186-1

12345 071 9876543

ACKNOWLEDGMENTS

Grateful acknowledgment is given to the following authors and publishers:

American Ethical Union for "We Sing of Golden Mornings" from *We Sing of Life*. Copyright © 1955: The American Ethical Union Library Catalog Number 54: 11625. Used by permission.

Atheneum Publishers, Inc., for "Wind Song" from *I Feel The Same Way* by Lilian Moore; text of *I Feel The Same Way*, copyright © 1967 by Lilian Moore. Used by permission.

Boosey & Hawkes, Inc., for "The Crow." "The Rook" (Song No. 2 from *Trois Petites Chansons*) by Igor Stravinsky. Copyright 1934 by Edition Russe de Musique (Russischer Musikverlag). © renewed 1961. Copyright and renewal assigned to Boosey & Hawkes, Inc. 1947. Used by permission.

Chappell Music Company for "Johnny One-Note." Copyright 1937 by Chappell & Co. Inc. Copyright renewed. International copyright secured. All rights reserved. Used by permission.

Chappell Music Company for "Woke Up This Morning," "Old Grey Mare," "Sow Took The Measles," and "The Streets of Glory." Copyright © 1975 by Chappell & Co. Inc. International copyright secured. All rights reserved. Used by permission.

Cherry Lane Music Co. for "The Music Is You" by John Denver. Copyright © 1974 by Cherry Lane Music Co. This arrangement copyright © 1980 by Cherry Lane Music Co. International copyright secured. All rights reserved. Used by permission.

Sharon Beth Falk for pattern arrangements to accompany "The Cuckoo" and "Kookaburra." Used by permission.

Carl Fischer, Inc., New York for "Waltzing Matilda." Copyright © 1966. Allans Music Australia Pty. Ltd. Copyright 1938. Used by permission.

Hansen Publications, Inc., for "The Campbells Are Comin'." Copyright © 1976 by Shattinger-International Music Corporation. Used by permission.

Hargall Music Press for "The Instruments" by Willy Geisler. Arranged by Julius Harford from *Humor In Vocal Music*. Copyright 1946 by Hargall Music Press. Used by permission.

Maclen Music, Inc., c/o ATV Music Corp., 6255 Sunset Blvd., Suite 723, Los Angeles, CA 90028, for "Yellow Submarine" (John Lennon and Paul McCartney) for the U.S.A., Canada, Mexico, and The Philippines; Northern Songs Limited for the rest of the world. Copyright © 1966 Maclen Music, Inc. All rights reserved. Used by permission.

Oxford University Press, Inc., for "Banana Boat Loader's Song" from *Folk Songs of Jamaica*. Copyright 1952 by Oxford University Press. Used by permission.

Paramount Music Corporation for "Jingle, Jangle, Jingle" by Frank Loesser and Joseph J. Lilley. Copyright 1942 by Paramount Music Corporation © renewed 1969 by Paramount Music Corporation. Used by permission.

Elena Paz for "Arruru." Copyright © 1971 by Elena Paz. Used by permission.

Peer International Corporation for "Sun Magic" and "Happiness Runs," a/k/a "Pebble and the Man." Copyright © 1968 by Donovan (Music) Ltd. Sole selling agent Peer International Corporation. Used by permission.

Theodore Presser Company and Oliver Ditson Company for "Goin' Home" from "Largo" of *Symphony No. 9 (From the New World)* by Antonin Dvořák. Arrangement copyright 1922 by Oliver Ditson Company. Used by permission.

G. Schirmer, Inc., for "March of the Kings" from *Christmas Carols from Many Lands*, translation by Satis Coleman. Copyright 1934 by G. Schirmer, Inc.; for "Marching to Pretoria," words by Josef Marais from *Songs From The Veld*. Copyright 1942 by G. Schirmer, Inc.; for "Laboring Song (No. 1)" from *Songs & Tales from the Dark Continent* by Natalie Curtis. Used by permission.

Schocken Books, Inc., for "Haynt Iz Purim, Brider" from *A Treasury of Jewish Folksongs* by Ruth Rubin. Copyright 1950 by Schocken Books, Inc., © renewed 1978 by Ruth Rubin. Used by permission.

Simon & Schuster, Inc., for "She'll Be Comin' Round the Mountain" and "Three Jolly Fishermen" from *The Fireside Book of Fun and Game Songs*. Collected and edited by Marie Winn. Musical arrangement by Allan Miller. Copyright © 1974 by Marie Winn and Allan Miller. Used by permission.

Paul Simon for "The 59th Street Bridge Song (Feelin' Groovy)" by Paul Simon. Copyright © 1966 by Paul Simon. All rights reserved. Used by permission.

Sing Out!—The Folksong Magazine for "Rock Island Line." Used by permission.

Summy-Birchard Company for "Weggis Dance" from *Birchard Music Series*, Book Four. Copyright © 1962 by Summy-Birchard Company. Used by permission.

Janet Tobitt for "De Bezem" from *The Ditty Bag*. Used by permission.

Charles E. Tuttle Co., Inc., for "Planting Rice" from *Folksongs Hawaii Sings*. Used by permission.

United States Committee for UNICEF for "Once" from Book 2 of the *Hi Neighbor Series*, published by the United States Committee for UNICEF, United Nations. Used by permission.

Warner Bros. Music for "Bye-Bye, Blackbird," Copyright 1926 by Warner Bros. Music. Copyright renewed. All rights reserved; for "I'm Looking Over A Four-Leaf Clover," Copyright 1927 by Warner Bros. Music. Copyright renewed. All rights reserved; for "A Swallow Song," Copyright © 1964 by Warner Bros. Music. All rights reserved. Used by permission.

World Around Songs for "When I Am Ten Years Old" from *Doing Nothing But Sing* and "Stars" from *For Happy Singing*. Used by permission.

PHOTO CREDITS

Unit Opener One   clockwise from left: A, B, D, E, HRW Photos by Russell Dian; C, HRW Photo by Ken Karp. Unit Opener Two p. 114 left, top right, HRW Photos by Ken Lax; bottom right, HRW Photo by Russell Dian.

HRW Photos by Russell Dian: p. 4 left, right; p. 22; p. 48; p. 72 bottom left; p. 73 bottom right; p. 76 percussion family, center top, right, bottom left, center; p. 128 top; p. 143; p. 196.

HRW Photos by Ken Karp: p. 4 center; p. 47 left; p. 56 left top; p. 72 top row; p. 73 top row, center left, bottom; p. 76 percussion family, top left; p. 181.

HRW Photos by Jim Kiernan: p. 3 top; p. 39; p. 50; p. 56 right top, center, bottom; p. 57 right top, center; p. 80; p. 114 bottom right; p. 118; p. 156; p. 177; p. 180; p. 185.

HRW Photos by Ken Lax: p. 37; p. 42; p. 56 left center, bottom; p. 57 left top, center; p. 59; p. 65; p. 72 banjo, timpani, violin; p. 73 bottom right; p. 74; p. 75; p. 76 brass family; p. 102; p. 178; p. 192; p. 193.
p. 57 bottom, Robert Frerck/Dimensions; p. 72 top center, courtesy of the Chinese Music Ensemble, N.Y.; bottom right, The Riverside Church; p. 72 center right, p. 73 bottom center, The Museum of the American Indian, Heye Foundation; p. 73 top left, courtesy of the Pro Musica Collection at New York University.

Additional copyright acknowledgments and photo credits appear with the materials used.

Illustrated by Susan Obrant, Eulala Conner, and Laurel Casazza.

Editorial Development   Lois Eskin, Alice Trimmer, Cathy Yudell
Editorial Processing   Margaret M. Byrne, Regina Chilcoat
Art and Production   Frank P. Lamacchia, Vivian Fenster, Fred C. Pusterla, Robin Swenson, Russell Dian, Paula Darmofal, Barbara Orzech, Anita Dickhuth, Ilene Cherna, Ellen Lokiec
Product Manager   J. Edward Johnson
Advisory Board   James Boyd, William G. Jones, David Joy, Sheila Nettles
Consultants   Sheila Nettles, Ruth Spies
Researchers   Eileen Kelly, Pamela Floch, Gerard LaVan

CONTENTS

MUSIC TO EXPLORE

THE MUSICIAN

THE MUSIC IS YOU

Words and Music by John Denver

Mu - sic makes_ pic - tures and of - ten tells_ sto -

- ries All of it_ mag - ic and all of it_ true._

_ And all of the pic - tures and all_

_ of the sto - ries And all of_ the

mag - ic, the mu - sic is_ you._

Which phrases of the melody are the **same**? Which are **different**?
Look at the chords given for each phrase.
Are they the **same**? **different**?
Could this song be performed as a round? How can you tell?

1

HAPPINESS RUNS

Words and Music by Donovan Leitch

Can you read in a circular motion?

How does this music express the idea of circular motion?

Hap-pi-ness runs in a cir-cu-lar mo-tion,

Thought is like a lit-tle boat up-on the sea.

You can have ev-'ry-thing if you let your-self be,

You can have ev-'ry-thing if you let your-self be.

MOVE IN A CIRCULAR MOTION
Jazz Walk

① 4/4

Doo   doo doo, Doo   doo doo,   Doo dah   doo dah!

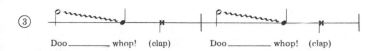

②

Doo   doo doo, Doo   doo doo,   Doo dah   doo dah!

③

Doo_____ whop! (clap)   Doo_____ whop! (clap)

④

Doo   doo doo, Doo   doo doo,   Doo dah   doo dah!

STAMPING GROUND

by Moondog

Can you hear . . .

melody

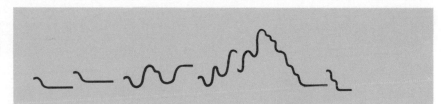

ostinato

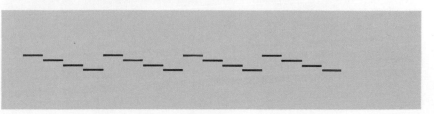

What part repeats the same pattern over and over?

3

ARE YOU SLEEPING?

Traditional Words

French Folk Tune

Sing this song in unison, then as a round.

1. **F**   **F**

Are   you   sleep - ing,   are   you   sleep - ing,

2. **F**   **F**

Broth - er   John,   Broth - er   John?

F   **F**

Morn - ing bells are ring - ing, morn - ing bells are ring - ing,

F   **F**

Ding,   ding,   dong,   ding,   ding,   dong.

Use the rhythm pattern of the words to create a percussion piece.
Some people may hold instruments while three players perform.

GROUP I	GROUP II	GROUP III
wood sounds	ringing sounds	thudding sounds

Perform the percussion piece as a three-part round.

4

Sing "Are You Sleeping?" in the following way. How many different ways is the melody varied?

① Slowly

Loo loo loo__ loo . . .

②

Perform the following parts as you sing.

INTRODUCTION *(2 meas.)* AND ACCOMPANIMENT

Piano or timpani

Alto Metallophone

Soprano Glockenspiel

SYMPHONY NO. 1 IN D MAJOR, (EXCERPT)

by Gustav Mahler

Listen to this music.
What do you hear that is the **same, almost the same,** or **different** from the way you performed "Are You Sleeping?" the first time?

5

SOUNDS OF FREEDOM

How many different kinds of freedom are there?
What does freedom "sound" like to you?

Use the sounds you have described to create a composition.
- Work in small groups.
- Choose a conductor.
- Make your composition about one minute long.
- Perform your compositions for one another.

- How did you feel about your composition?
- What in the music made you feel that way?
- Would you like to change your composition?

MOVE TO SPECIAL IDEAS IN MUSIC

SEMPER FIDELIS

by John Philip Sousa

Introduction . . . GET READY TO MOVE!	
A A	Will you move with the **even** rhythm played by the low brass and percussion?
	OR
	Will you move with the **uneven** rhythm played by the high brass and woodwinds?
B B	Listen to the melody played by the woodwinds and high brass. Will you move with even or uneven motions?
Interlude	Can you follow the rhythm of the snare drum?
C	Will you move with smooth or jagged motions?
LOW BRASS	
C' C'	What has been added? Move with its sound!
D D	Choose the instrument you like best. Move with it!

WOKE UP THIS MORNING

1960's U.S. Civil Rights Movement

1. I woke up this morn-ing with my mind,___ it was
2. ⅞ Walk-in' and talk-in' with my mind,___ it was

stayed_____ on free - dom,_ I
stayed_____ on free - dom,_ ⅞

woke up this morn-ing with my mind,___ it was
Walk-in' and talk-in' with my mind,___ it was

stayed_____ on free - dom,_ I
stayed_____ on free - dom,_ ⅞

woke up this morn-ing with my mind,___ it was
Walk-in' and talk-in' with my mind,___ it was

stayed _____ on free - dom,_ Hal-le- lu,_
stayed _____ on free - dom,_ Hal-le- lu,_

_____ Hal - le - lu,_ _____ Ha - le -
_____ Hal - le - lu,_ _____ Ha - le -

lu - - jah! _____
lu - - jah! _____

Midnight Ride of Paul Revere, 1931, Grant Wood (1892-1942, United States) Oil on composition board, 30" x 40".
The Metropolitan Museum of Art, New York. Courtesy Associated American Artists, Inc., New York.

A DREAM

Excerpts from the Gettysburg Address

Dreamer: One night I dreamed of a great nation!
In my dream, voices said:

Solo I: "Four score and seven years ago our fathers
brought forth on this continent a new nation . . ."

Solo II: And this new nation was "conceived in liberty . . ."

Dreamer: Does this mean liberty and freedom for *all* people?

Group I	**Group II**
Yes!	Even freedom of thought?
Yes!	Freedom to choose?
Yes!	Freedom to speak out?
Yes!	

Dreamer: Ah . . . but with freedom comes responsibility!

Group I	**Group II**
Yes! Responsibility . . .	for thought.
Responsibility . . .	for choices.
Responsibility . . .	for actions.
And responsibility . . .	to each other.

Dreamer: How could such a nation possibly work?

Solo I: The **people** make it happen.

Solo II: The people?

Group I: The **people!**   **Group II:** The **people!**

Dreamer: One night I dreamed of a great nation . . .

MEMORY GAME 1

How well can you remember what you see?
Play the following games to find out!

- Look at this design while you count to ten.
- Cover it with a blank card.

- Look at this design.
- Cover both designs.
- Are the two designs the **same**? **similar**? **different**?
- Uncover both designs.
- Was your answer correct?

- Take your card and cover the left half of the painting on page 12.
- Look at the part of the painting that is not covered.
- Slide the card across the page.
  Look at the other half of the painting.
- Are the two halves of the painting the **same**, **similar**, or **different**?

- Try the same test with the painting on page 13.

New York City I, 1942, Piet Mondrian (1872–1948, The
Netherlands) Oil on canvas, 47″ × 45″. Courtesy Sidney
Janis Gallery, New York.

Roumanian Blouse, 1940, Henri Matisse (1869-1954, France)
Oil on canvas, 36¼" × 28¾". Musée d'Art Moderne, Paris,
France. © S.P.A.D.E.M., 1978.

13

MEMORY GAME 2

How well can you remember what you hear?
Can you hear two melodies and then decide if they are the **same,**
similar, or **different**?

- You will hear a melody.
- Then you will hear a second melody.
- Are these two musical ideas the **same,**

    similar,

    or **different?**

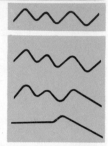

- Listen to a melody.
- Sing what you have heard.
- Listen to a second melody. Sing it!
- Are the ideas the **same, similar,** or **different?**

- Listen to a musical idea.
- "Think" the melody you heard.
- Listen to a second melody. "Think" it.
- Are the melodies the **same, similar,** or **different?**

- Think of a song you know very well.
- Everyone sing it together.
- Sing it a second time. This time sing the song "silently" except for the last word in each phrase.
- Does everyone sing the last word together?

DOWN AND OUT

Traditional Blues

1. Tired and wear-y,   I got the blues. _____
2. Boss just fired me,   More bad news. _____
3. Down and out, —   I got the blues. _____

Tired and wear-y,   I got the blues. _____
Boss just fired me,   More bad news. _____
Down and out, —   I got the blues. _____

Down and   out, —   Those same old   blues. _____
He didn't want me,   Those same old   blues. _____
No am - bi-tion,   Those same old   blues. _____

THE RIDDLE SONG

American Folk Song

G   **C**   **C**   **G**

1. I gave my love a cher-ry that has no stone;
2. How can there be a cher-ry that has no stone?
3. A cher-ry when it's bloom-ing, it has no stone;

D7   **G**   **G**   **Am**

I gave my love a chick-en that has no _ bone;
How can there be a chick-en that has no _ bone?
A chick-en when it's pip-ping, it has no _ bone;

D7   **G**   **G**   **D7**

I gave my love a ring _ that has no _ end;
How can there be a ring _ that has no _ end?
A ring _ when it's roll-ing it has no _ end;

Am   **C**   **C**   **G**

I gave my love a ba-by, there's no cry-en.
How can there be a ba-by, there's no cry-en?
A ba-by when it's sleep-ing, there's no cry-en.

16

■ MEMORY GAME 3 ■

Brush up on your listening skills!

G
A
M
E

- Listen to the first part of a composition.
  You may hear it several times if you wish.

- Listen to the complete composition.
  As you listen, decide:
- How many parts are in the composition?
- Which parts are the **same** as the first?

- Write down your answer.

- Check yourself by looking at the music.

Triptych: Landscape, c. 1910–1919, Louis C. Tiffany (1848–
1933, United States) Stained glass window. Art Museum,
Princeton University, New Jersey. Gift of Norman A. Ballantine.

17

BYE-BYE, BLACKBIRD

Words by Mort Dixon

Music by Ray Henderson

Pack up all my care and woe,

Here I go sing - ing low,

Bye Bye Black - bird, _____

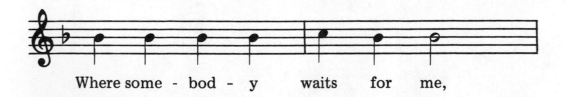

Where some - bod - y waits for me,

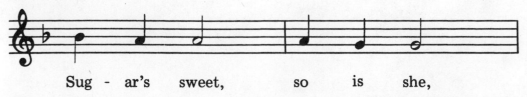

Sug - ar's sweet, so is she,

Bye   Bye   Black - bird. _____

No one here can love and un - der - stand   me,

Oh what hard luck sto - ries they all   hand   me;

Make   my   bed   and   light   the   light,

I'll   ar - rive   late   to - night,

Black - bird _____ Bye   Bye. _____

MUSIC FROM LOUISIANA STORY

by Virgil Thomson

You can remember the **A** section of a short song
and recognize it when it returns.
Can you stretch your musical memory to remember the
A section when you hear a long instrumental composition?

PAPA'S TUNE

from Acadian Songs and Dances

Begin by playing the theme several times.

- Listen to the composition.
  Decide how many sections you hear.
- Draw one box for each section on a piece of paper.
  Write an "A" in the first box.
- Listen again! Write a letter in each box.
  Write "A" if you hear the first theme again.
  Write "B" if you hear a different theme.

20

CHORALE (THE DERRICK ARRIVES)

**excerpt
from Louisiana Story (Suite)**

Follow the same steps as you listen to "Chorale." Begin by playing the theme.

THE ALLIGATOR AND THE 'COON

from Acadian Songs and Dances

This composition is much longer.
Can you still keep the **A** theme in mind?

Check Point I

Can you . . .
  perform
     describe
        compose
- an **ostinato** to go with a melody?
- **major** melodies . . . **minor** melodies?
- **same, similar,** and **different** sections?

THE
MUSICIAN

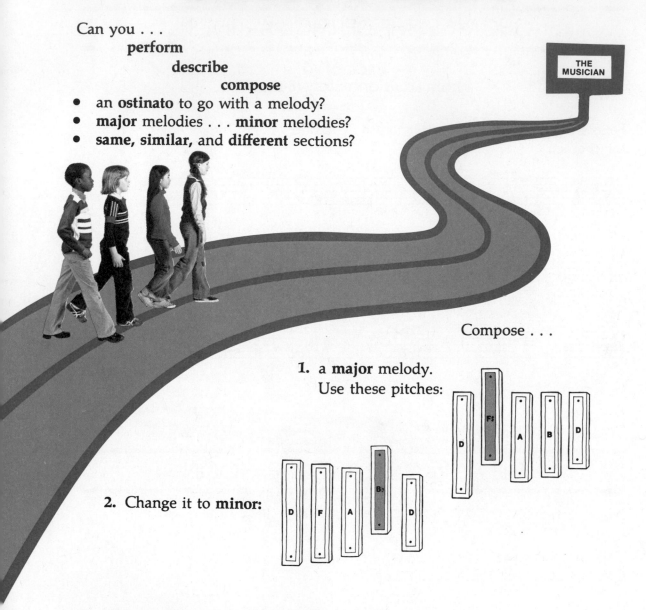

Compose . . .

1. a **major** melody.
Use these pitches:

D   F♯   A   B   D

2. Change it to **minor:**

D   F   A   B♭   D

3. Add an **ostinato** to your melody.

4. Plan a design for your composition
that is the same as one of the
works of art on pages 9, 12, 13, or 17.

DESCRIBE...

- each other's compositions
- music you hear

PERFORM...

- "Where Is John?" in **major**
- change it to **minor**
- sing one part as an **ostinato**

WHERE IS JOHN?

Czechoslovakian Folk Song

Where is   John?__ The old   red hen   has   left   her pen.

Where is   John?__ The cows   are   in   the   corn   a - gain.

Oh, John! _____

FOLLOW THE TONAL CENTER

Most melodies have a **tonal center.** The **tonal center** is the pitch to which the melody returns.

Listen to "The Three Fishermen." Notice how it keeps returning to the **tonal center.**

Listen again. This time, sing the **tonal center** on "loo" each time the melody returns to that pitch.

THE THREE FISHERMEN

Traditional

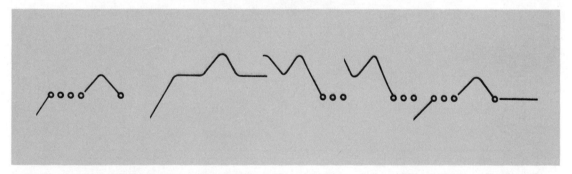

Now sing the song with words.

> There were three jol-ly fish-er-men.
> There were three jol-ly fish-er-men.
> Fish-er, fish-er, men, men, men.
> Fish-er, fish-er, men, men, men.
> There were three jol-ly fish-er-men.

Listen to a familiar song.
The **tonal center** has been omitted.

- Can you sing that pitch each time you see a circle?

SHE'LL BE COMIN' ROUND
THE MOUNTAIN

Traditional

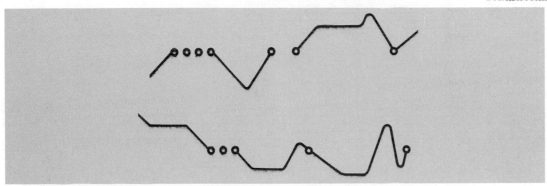

Here's another song you know. Play this game!

- Sing only the words that sound on the **tonal center**.
- "Think" all the other pitches.

Can you sing the right pitch each time the melody returns to the **tonal center**?

Notice that this song has both a HIGH and a LOW **tonal center**.

ROW, ROW, ROW YOUR BOAT

Traditional Round

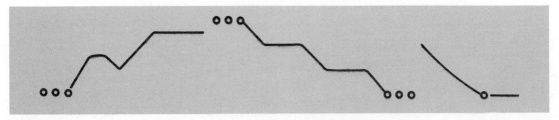

JOHNNY ONE-NOTE

Words by Lorenz Hart

Music by Richard Rodgers

John-ny could on-ly sing one note And the note he sang was this:

Ah _____

1. Poor John-ny   One - Note_ Sang out_with gus-to_And
2. Poor John-ny   One - Note_ Got in_ A - i - da, In-

just   o - ver - lord - ed_ the   place._____
deed   a_ great   chance to_ be   brave._____

Poor John-ny One-Note_Yelled   wil - ly - nil - ly,_   Un-
He took his   one note, Howled like the North Wind,_Brought

til he was blue in the face,_____ For
forth wind that made crit-ics rave,_____ While

hold - ing one note was his ace._____Could-n't hear the
Ver - di turned round in his grave!_____Could-n't hear the

brass,_____ Could-n't hear the drum,_____ He was in a
flute_____ or the big trom - bone_____ Ev-'ry-one was

class_____ By him-self, by gum!_____
mute,_____ John-ny stood a - lone._____

Sing John-ny One-Note, Sing out with gus - to And

just o - ver - whelm all the crowd._____

Ah!_____ So

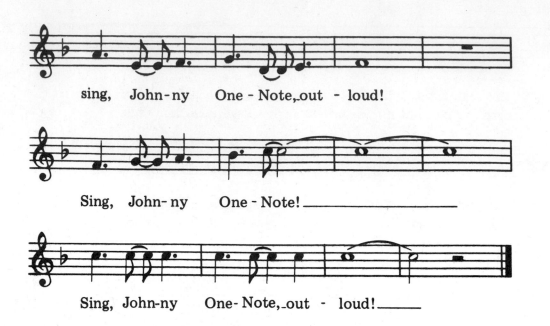

sing, John-ny One - Note, out - loud!

Sing, John- ny One - Note! _____

Sing, John-ny One- Note, out - loud! _____

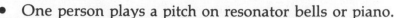

MEMORY GAME 4

Good tonal memory will help you learn new songs more easily.
Try these games to help you improve.

- One person plays a pitch on resonator bells or piano.
- Everyone hums that pitch, then "thinks" it.
- A leader counts silently to eight, then points to someone.
- Can that person sing the pitch out loud?

- Can you still remember the pitch if there is a distraction?
- The leader will play the pitch.
  Then you will hear a rhythm.
- Can you still sing the pitch?

• LEADER PLAYS	• ALL HUM	• LEADER CLAPS	• ALL CLAP	• SOMEONE SINGS

- This time, the distraction will be a melody.
- Can you still sing the **tonal center** when the leader points to you?

• LEADER PLAYS	• ALL HUM	• LEADER plays a tune using any of these pitches.	• SOMEONE SINGS

AMERICA, THE BEAUTIFUL

Words by Katharine Lee Bates

Music by Samuel A. Ward

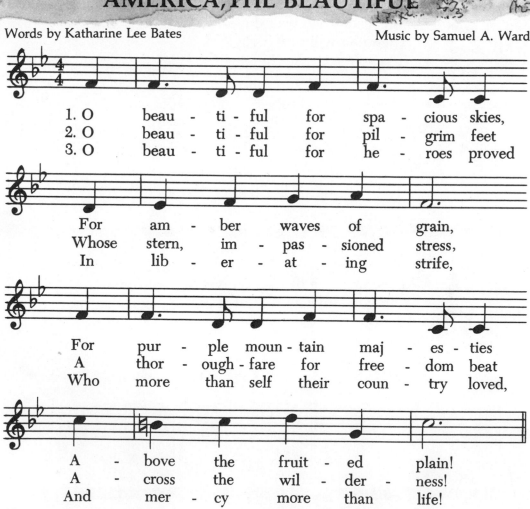

1. O   beau - ti - ful   for   spa - cious skies,
2. O   beau - ti - ful   for   pil - grim feet
3. O   beau - ti - ful   for   he - roes proved

For   am - ber   waves   of   grain,
Whose   stern,   im - pas - sioned   stress,
In   lib - er - at - ing   strife,

For   pur - ple moun - tain   maj - es - ties
A   thor - ough-fare   for   free - dom beat
Who   more   than self   their   coun - try loved,

A - bove   the   fruit - ed   plain!
A - cross   the   wil - der - ness!
And   mer - cy   more   than   life!

A - mer - i - ca, A - mer - i - ca,
A - mer - i - ca, A - mer - i - ca,
A - mer - i - ca, A - mer - i - ca,

God shed his grace on thee,
God mend thine ev - ery flaw,
May God thy gold re - fine,

And crown thy good with broth - er - hood
Con - firm thy soul in self - con - trol,
Till all suc - cess be no - ble - ness,

From sea to shin - ing sea.
Thy lib - er - ty in law.
And ev - ery gain di - vine.

TONAL-CENTER TUNE-UP TIME

Keeping the **tonal center** in mind will help you to learn a new melody. Begin by using a **tonal-center** tune up.

Tune up: 1 3 3 1 7, 2 7, 1 3 3 1
F   5   5,   5,   5

- Can you sing each of the following melody patterns?
- Can you always return "home" to "1," the **tonal center**?

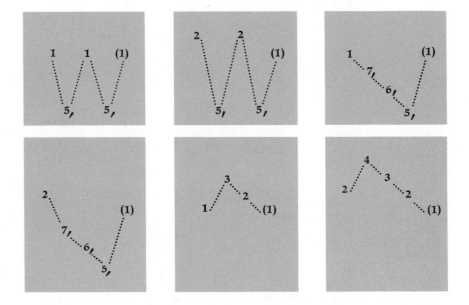

Here are the same patterns in musical notation.

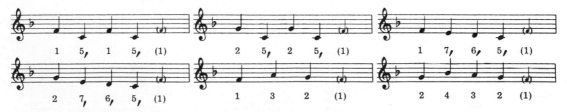

1 5, 1 5, (1)   2 5, 2 5, (1)   1 7, 6, 5, (1)

2 7, 6, 5, (1)   1 3 2 (1)   2 4 3 2 (1)

These patterns make up the song "Who Did?"
Can you sing them in the order of the song shown on page 33?
Remember to keep the **tonal center** in mind!

WHO DID?

Traditional

1. Who did, who did, who did, who did, Who did swal - low Jo, Jo, Jo, Jo? *
2. Whale did, whale did, whale did, whale did, Whale did swal - low Jo, Jo, Jo, Jo;

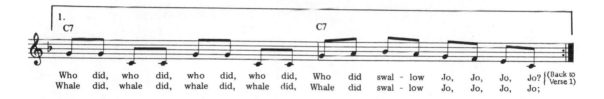

1.

Who did, who did, who did, who did, Who did swal - low Jo, Jo, Jo, Jo? {(Back to Verse 1)

Whale did, whale did, whale did, whale did, Whale did swal - low Jo, Jo, Jo, Jo;

2.

Who did swal-low Jo - nah? Who did swal-low Jo - nah? Who did swal-low Jo - nah   down?

Whale did swal-low Jo - nah; Whale did swal-low Jo - nah, Whale did swal-low Jo - nah   down.

3.   Ga-briel . . . blow your trum - - - pet   loud!

4.   Dan - iel . . . in the li - - - ions' den!

Practice learning other new songs by singing **scale numbers** in relation to the **tonal center**.

- Choose a song from page 115, 134, or 136.
- Tune up.
- Then sing the song with numbers.
- Listen to the recording to see if you were correct.

HOME, SWEET HOME

Make up a melody for this poem. Return to the **tonal center** each time the word "Home" appears.

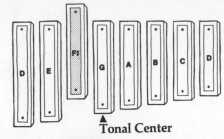

Tonal Center

HOME, SWEET HOME

Home, sweet home,
I really like my home.
I go to school each day,
But home is where I play.
What fun to be back home!

Home Again

Write your own poem. Include some of these words:

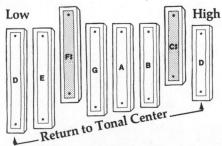

HOME POEM ROAM COMB DOME CHROME

Make up a melody. Return "home" when you use these words.

Low   High

D E F♯ G A B C♯ D

Return to Tonal Center

CHANGING TONAL CENTERS

Composers can add interest to their music by changing the **tonal center.**
Listen again to "The Alligator and the 'Coon."
- Can you hear when the **tonal center** changes?
- Follow this map as you listen.
- Point to a new box each time the **tonal center** moves.

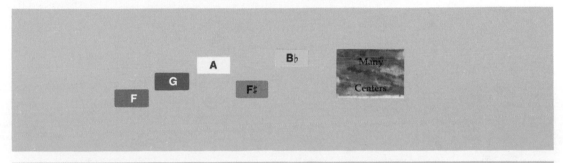

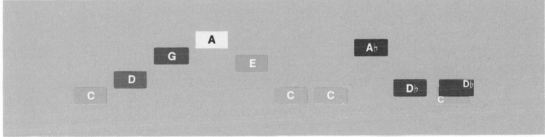

Did you have trouble hearing the **tonal center** at the end?
That was because each trumpet has its own **tonal center.**
Try playing their tune in two **tonal centers** at the same time!

PLAYER 1

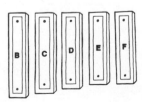

PLAYER 2

35

DE BEZEM

Dutch Round

Tune up:
$$\begin{matrix} & & 5 \\ & 3 & \ 3 \\ 1 & & \ 1 \\ E\flat & & \end{matrix}$$

Sing this song using **scale numbers.**
Then listen to the recording
to learn the Dutch words.

1. De be - zem, de be - zem,

2. Wat doe je er mee? Wat doe je er mee?

3. Wij ve - gen er mee, Wij ve - gen er mee,

4. De vloer aan, de vloer aan!

Form four groups.
Each group sings a different phrase of the song.
All four groups sing at the same time.

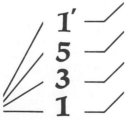

- What happened?

36

JOHNNY! JOHNNY!

Traditional Canon

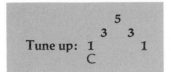

Tune up: 1 3 3 5 1
C

Learn to sing this song.

1. John-ny!   John-ny!   2.   Well!   Well!

Here we come sing-ing and here we come call-ing and

- Look at the musical notation.
- Decide which pitches you will need to create a chordal accompaniment for this song.
- Select your pitches from these bells:

- Accompany this song with **chords** using the bells you chose. How many different **chords** did you play?

37

GOING HOME

Adaptation of words by
William Arms Fisher

Music by Antonin Dvořák

Listen to the recording of this song.
Can you hear the I chord begin and end the music?

1.   Go - ing home, go - ing home, I'm a - go - ing home;___
      Moth-er's there ex-pect-ing me, Father's wait - ing too;___
2.   Morn-ing star   lights the way, Rest-less dream all done;___
      Go - ing home,   go - ing home, I'm just go - ing home;___

Qui - et - like, some still day, I'm just go - ing   home._
Lots of folk gath-er'd there, All the friends I   knew._
Shad-ows gone, break of day, Real life just be - gun.___
It's not far, just close by, Through an o - pen door._

It's not far,   just close by, Through an o - pen door;_
There's no break, there's no end, Just a - liv - ing on;___

D.C. al Fine

Work all done, care laid by, Going to fear no more._
Wide a - wake, with a smile, Go - ing on and on.___

Although the harmony begins and ends on the I chord, you also hear other chords. Can you hear when the harmony returns to the **I chord**? Show it!
- Move to express the feelings of the whole song.
- Move only when you hear the I chord.
  Freeze when you hear the other chords.

Divide into two groups.
- **Group I** moves only with the I chord.
- **Group II** moves only with the other sounds of chordal harmony.
  How did the harmony help express the idea of the words?

SYMPHONY NO. 9 IN E MINOR, "NEW WORLD"

Largo (excerpt)   by Antonin Dvořák

Listen to an orchestra play the melody you just sang.
What differences do you notice between this composition and "Going Home"?
Is the harmony the **same** or **different**?

LA JESUSITA

English Words Adapted   Mexican Folk Song

Look at these pictures of the melody and harmony of this song.

- Will the melody begin below, on, or above the **tonal center**?
- How will it end?
- How many different chords does this song use?
- Listen to the recording. Can you hear when the chords change?

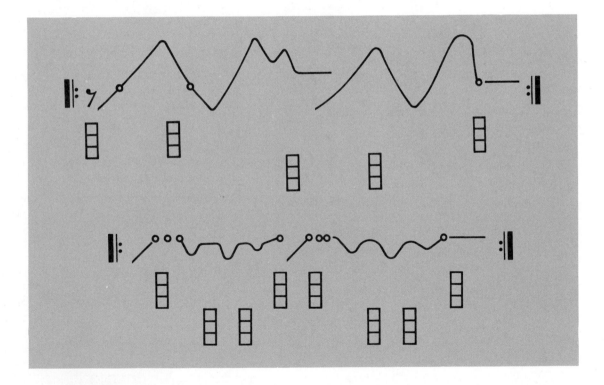

Come let us dance where the lan-terns shine bright-ly, _____
Va - mos al bai - le y ve - rás ¡qué bo - ni - to! _____

Come let us join in the fun step-ping light-ly. ____
don - de se a - lum - bran con vein - te lin - ter - nas, ____

Down in the square where the danc-ers are swing-ing _____
don - de se bai - lan las dan - zas mo - der - nas, _____

And all the lat - est of steps can be seen. Tra la la la!
don - de se bai - la de mu-cho va-ci - lón. Ya-ya-ya-ya!

Oh, dance with me, Je - su - si - ta,
Y quié - re - me, Je - su - si - ta,

Oh, please, won't you dance with me?
y quié - re - me por fa - vor.

If you'll be my danc - ing part - ner,
Y mi - ra que soy tu a - man - te,

Then your faith - ful slave I'll be.
y se - gu - ro ser - vi - dor.

LOVELY EVENING

Traditional Round

Play this chord sequence on the autoharp.

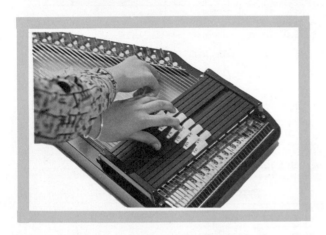 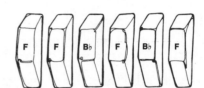

Listen to this song.
How often do you hear the chord sequence you just played?
Accompany the song. It moves in groups of three.
● Will you play a chord on every beat in the measure?
   on only the first beat? the last?

1. Oh, how love-ly is the eve-ning, is the eve-ning,

2. When the bells are sweet-ly ring-ing, sweet-ly ring-ing.

3. Ding, dong, ding, dong, ding, dong.

THE RAILROAD CORRAL

Cowboy Song

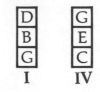

I   IV

This song uses two chords.
Begin with the **G** chord.
When does your ear tell you the chord should change?
Accompany this song using autoharp, ukulele, or guitar.

1. We're up   in   the morn - ing   ere break - ing   of day,
2. Come take   up   your cin - ches, come shake out   your reins,

The chuck wag - on's bus - y,   the flap - jack's in   play.
Come wake your   old bron - co   and break for   the plains;

The herd   is a - stir   o - ver hill - side   and vale,
Come roust   out your   steers from   the long chap - ar - ral,

With the   night rid - ers crowd - ing   them in - to   the trail.
For the out - fit   is off   to   the rail - road cor - ral.

43

POLLY WOLLY DOODLE

American Folk Song

Here is another two-chord song.
Learn the melody.
Then add an accompaniment on the autoharp.
Use your ears and eyes to decide when to change from the

I chord [C A F] to the V7 chord [Bb G E C]

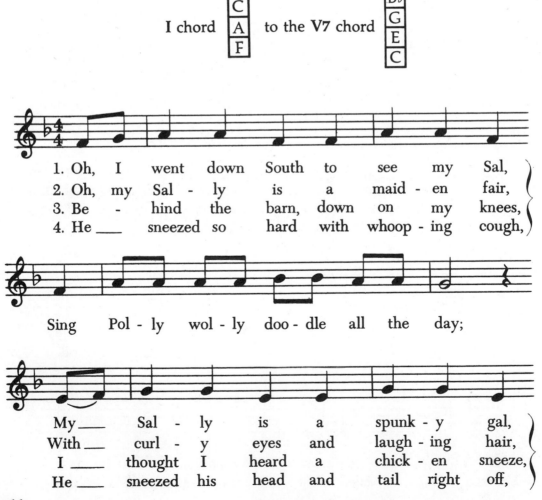

1. Oh, I went down South to see my Sal,
2. Oh, my Sal - ly is a maid - en fair,
3. Be - hind the barn, down on my knees,
4. He ___ sneezed so hard with whoop - ing cough,

Sing Pol - ly wol - ly doo - dle all the day;

My ___ Sal - ly is a spunk - y gal,
With ___ curl - y eyes and laugh - ing hair,
I ___ thought I heard a chick - en sneeze,
He ___ sneezed his head and tail right off,

Sing Pol - ly wol - ly doo - dle all the day.

Refrain

Fare thee well, fare thee well, Fare thee

well, my fair - y fay, For I'm

going to Loui - si - an - a, for to see my Su - sy - an - na,

Sing Pol - ly wol - ly doo - dle all the day.

You can also add a vocal accompaniment to this song!
Divide into two groups.
Group I sings the melody.
Group II sings the **root,** the first pitch, of each chord.

Sing this for
the **I** chord.

Sing this for
the **V7** chord.

Oh, I went down South . . .

. . . day.

CRAWDAD SONG

American Folk Song

This song uses three chords. Listen to the recording several times.
Hold up one finger when you hear the **I chord.**
Fold your arms when you hear different chords.
Use the autoharp to decide whether the different chords should be   or

C	B♭	F
A	G	D
F	E	B♭
I	C	

1.   You get a line and I'll get a pole, Hon-ey,
2. Yon-der comes a man with a sack on his back, Hon-ey,
3. What-cha gon-na do when the lake runs dry, Hon-ey?

You get a line and I'll get a pole, Babe,
Yon-der comes a man with a sack on his back, Babe,
What-cha gon-na do when the lake runs dry, Babe?

You get a line and I'll get a pole,
Yon-der comes a man with a sack on his back,
What-cha gon-na do when the lake runs dry?

We'll go down to the craw - dad hole,____
Tot-in' all the craw - dads he can pack,____
Sit on the bank and watch the craw-dads die,____

Hon-ey,   Babe,_   mine.
Hon-ey,   Babe,_   mine.
Hon-ey,   Babe,_   mine.

FLOP-EARED MULE

Listen to this piece played on two folk instruments:

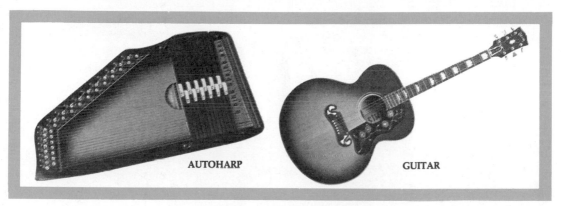

AUTOHARP   GUITAR

These two instruments sound very much alike.
- Can you hear the melody played on the autoharp?

Listen again.
Clap this pattern:

The chordal harmony uses this pattern throughout most
of the piece. Can you follow along as the chords change?

Play tones from these chords on bells as you hear the music.
- Which bells will you need?

47

Check Point II

Can you . . .

- hear and remember the **tonal center**?
- learn a melody using **scale numbers**?
- show the relationship of the shortest sound to longer sounds?
- recognize when chords change?

THE MUSICIAN

WHEN I AM TEN YEARS OLD

Norwegian Folk Song

Verse

1. When I am ten years old,
2. When I am twen-ty years old, Boom fa la la la, Boom fa le lay,
3. When I am thir-ty years old,

48

Then I to school must go,⎫
Then I a-court-in' go, ⎬Boom fa la la la lay.
I wear a band of gold,⎭

Refrain

When I am ten years old,
When I am twen-ty years old,
When I am thir-ty years old,

Then I to school must go.⎫
Then I a - court - in' go. ⎬
I wear a band of gold.⎭

Boom fa la fa la, Boom fa le lay, Boom fa la la la

lay. Cho Hey.

4.   When I am forty years old, Oh, how my family grows.
5.   When I am fifty years old, My hair is gray and gold.
6.   When I am sixty years old, My hair is white as snow.
7.   When I am seventy years old, I have no hair at all.
8.   When I am eighty years old, Oh, how the backache grows.
9.   When I am ninety years old, Then I to Heaven go.
10. When I am a hundred years old, I wear two wings of gold.
11. When I am a thousand years old,
     Oh, how my spirits roam. (*whisper*)

- Accompany this song with bells.
- Use these chords.
  When will you change to each chord?

A		D		G
F#		B		E
D		G		C#
				A
I		IV		V⁷

PADDY WORKS ON THE RAILWAY

American Work Song

Listen to this work song.
Perform a dance with the music as though you were the
workers. Begin by walking to work.
With hands in your back pockets . . . walk in a circle.

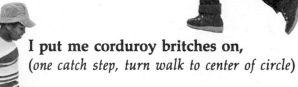

In eighteen hundred and forty one,
(*walk in swaggering style in a circle*)

I put me corduroy britches on,
(*one catch step, continue walking in circle*)

I put me corduroy britches on,
(*one catch step, turn walk to center of circle*)

To work upon the railway.
(*step backwards out of circle*)

Fil-i-mee-oo-re-i-re-ay,
(*pantomime swinging heavy sledge
hammer on* **accented** *syllables*)

Fil-i-mee-oo-re-i-re-ay,

Fil-i-mee-oo-re-i-re-ay,

To work upon the railway.
(*catch step, pivot in circle*)

- Which were the **accented** syllables?

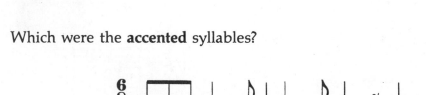

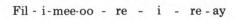

Fil - i - mee-oo - re - i - re - ay

MAKE NEW FRIENDS

Traditional Round

Here are two ways to sing this song. Learn both ways.

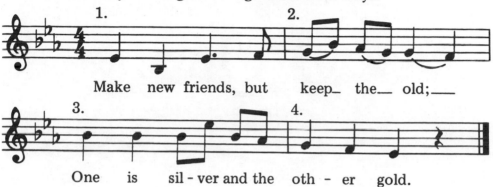

Make new friends, but keep_ the_ old;___

One is sil - ver and the oth - er gold.

John - ny, Jo - seph, Pen - ny, Paul, Na -

than - iel, Mat - thew, James and Raul, Ra -

- mo - na, Cin - dy, Don - nie, Su - san,

I've a lot of friends this fall.

- Which song moves with the shortest sound most of the time?

51

MEASURE A RHYTHM

- How long is each sound in this song?
  Make a ruler to match the one at the bottom of page 53.
  Place it under each row of rhythm.
- Measure each sound.
- Can you describe the length of each sound?

ONCE

Israeli Folk Song

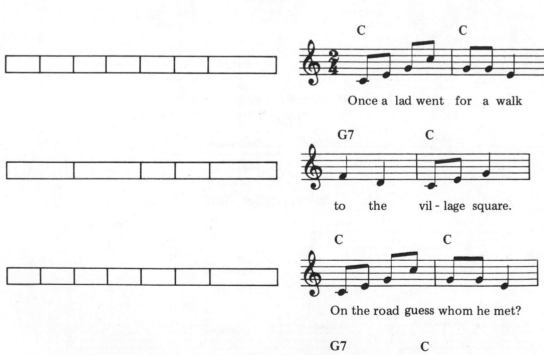

Once a lad went for a walk

to the vil - lage square.

On the road guess whom he met?

A young maid - en fair.

This is the rhythm of the first phrase of "The Three Fishermen."

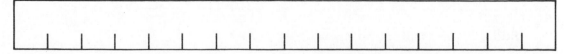

Use your ruler to draw the rhythm of the other phrases.

A Rhythm Ruler

Copy this rhythm ruler.
Put it on oaktag or construction paper.

HEY, HO! ANYBODY HOME?

English Round

Can you learn this rhythm?
- Tap the **shortest sound** on your knee.
- Chant the rhythm with "choo."

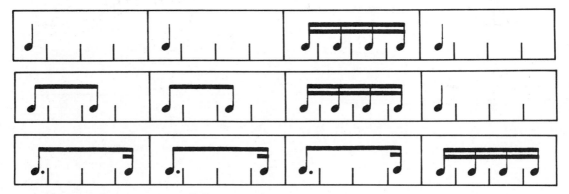

Perform the rhythm of this song with the words.
- Can you follow the notes on the staff?
- Which note equals the **shortest sound**?

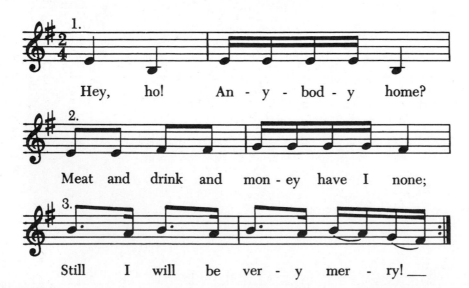

1. Hey, ho! An - y - bod - y home?

2. Meat and drink and mon - ey have I none;

3. Still I will be ver - y mer - ry! __

54

IFCA'S CASTLE

Traditional Round

- Which note equals the **shortest sound**?
- How many short sounds does each other note equal?

1. 2.
A - bove the plain of gold and green,

3. 4.
A young boy's head is plain - ly seen;

5. 6.
A hu - ya, hu - ya, hu - ya - ya, Swift - ly flow - ing riv - er,

7. 8.
A hu - ya, hu - ya, hu - ya - ya, Swift - ly flow - ing riv - er.

SOUND TOGETHER

- Work in pairs.
- Choose one of these ideas.
- One person sets up a steady rhythm
  that moves in groups of four.
- The other person makes up movements to match the rhythm.

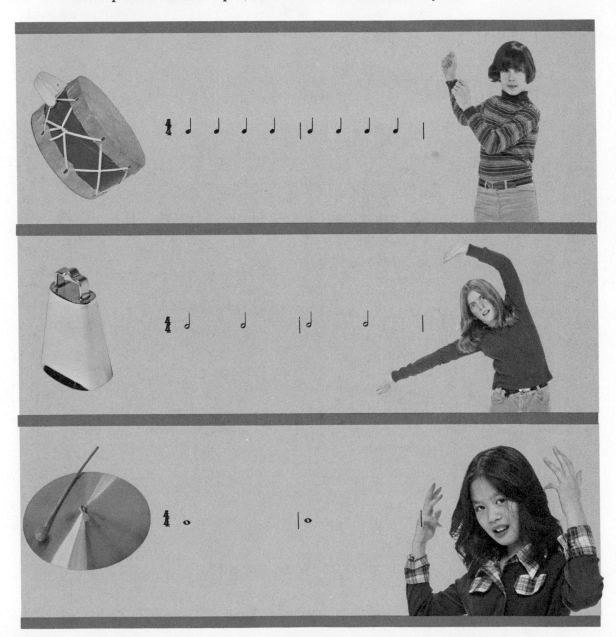

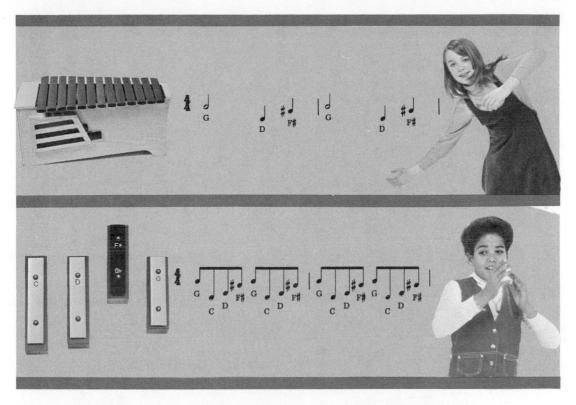

When each pair has planned its part, put them all together in an **ensemble.**

TJARABALEN

Listen! Do you hear any of the patterns you played?

Javanese Folk Melody

MUSICAL DECISIONS

Use your musical skills to learn this song.
1. Learn the **rhythm** and the **melody.**
2. Add **harmony** on bass xylophone.
   Use these pitches: A G F E D

A SWALLOW SONG

Words and music by Richard Fariña

1. Come wan - der qui-et - ly, and
2.   is no sor-row like the

lis - ten to the wind. Come near and lis - ten to the
mur - mur of their wings, There is no choir — like their

sky. ___ Come walk-ing high a-bove the roll-ing of the sea, And
song. ___ There is no pow-er like the free-dom of their flight, —

watch the swal-lows as they fly. 2. There
While the swal-lows roam a -   - lone.

When a performer has learned the melody, rhythm, and harmony
of a song, there are still many musical decisions to make.
- Can you think of some of the decisions a performer needs to
  make in order to perform a song expressively?

58

TEMPO: A MUSICAL DECISION

Metronome

The numbers tell the number
of beats per minute.
The tick equals the length of one **beat-note.**

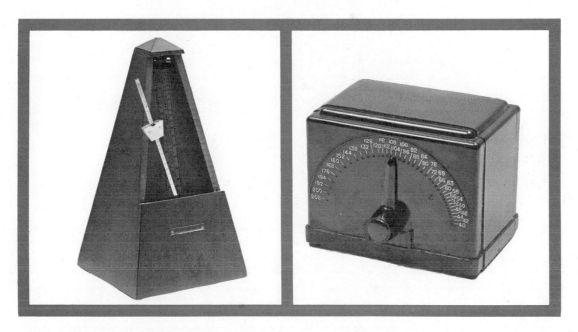

One decision a musician must make is related to **tempo.**
How fast or slow should music be performed?
• How will you decide the **tempo?**
Composers or arrangers sometimes give the **tempo** in the musical
score. It may be shown in one of these three ways:

English Words	Italian Words	Metronome Markings
very slow	*largo*	about 60
moderately slow	*adagio*	about 90
moderate	*andante*	about 120
fast	*allegro*	about 160
very fast	*presto*	about 180 or more!

BE A HUMAN "METRONOME"

To set your own tempo, try these ideas.

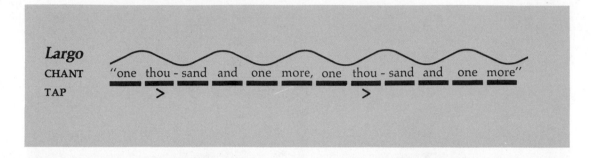

Largo
CHANT   "one thou - sand and one more, one thou - sand and one more"
TAP   >   >

Adagio
CHANT   "one thou - sand one, one thou - sand one"
TAP   >   >

A TIMELY RHYME

Anonymous

Set a largo tempo. ♩ = 60   Set an adagio tempo. ♩ = 90
Chant the rhyme.   Chant the rhyme.

Try other tempos. Which fits the mood of the words?

The   time of day I do not tell as some do by the clock,
Or   by the dis-tant chim-ing bell set   on some steep-led rock;
But   by the pro-gress that I see in what I have to   do,
It's   ei-ther "done-o-clock" for me, or on - ly "half-past through."

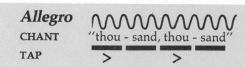

Andante
CHANT "one thou-sand, one thou-sand"
TAP

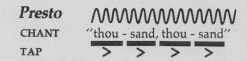

Allegro
CHANT "thou-sand, thou-sand"
TAP

Presto
CHANT "thou-sand, thou-sand"
TAP

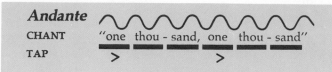

THE BELL DOTH TOLL

Traditional Round

Try this song in each tempo.
Which do you think is best?   ♩ = one beat

The bell doth toll, its ech - oes roll, I know the sound full well,

I love its ring - ing, for it calls to sing - ing

With its bim, bim, bim, bom, bell.   Bim, bom, bim, bom, bell.

61

ARTICULATION: A MUSICAL DECISION

Another musical decision a musician must make is related
to **articulation**.
How should each sound be performed?
How will each sound begin? end? move to the next?
- How will *you* decide the **articulation**?

Can you perform these sounds?
- How will you start each sound? stop it? progress to the next?

These are some terms used to describe musical **articulation**.
- Can you decide what each word means by looking at the symbols?

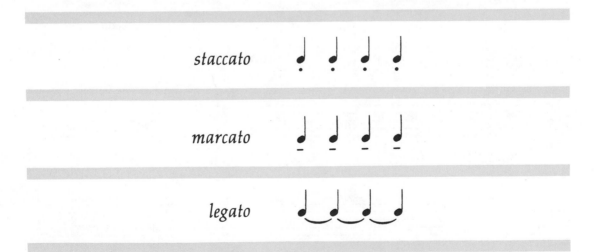

staccato

marcato

legato

How will you **articulate** the sounds when you sing:
"A Swallow Song"
"Happiness Runs"
"Woke Up This Morning"
- Will you sing the same way through the whole song?

DYNAMICS: A MUSICAL DECISION

A third musical decision a musician must make is related to **dynamics.**

*   How loud or soft should a song be?
*   Should it grow louder? grow softer?

Sometimes the dynamics are given in the musical score. The performer must still decide:

*   How soft is *piano* (*p*)? *pianissimo* (*pp*)? *mezzo piano* (*mp*)?
*   How loud is *forte* (*f*)? *fortissimo* (*ff*)? *mezzo forte* (*mf*)?

Practice controlling the dynamic level of a drum or your voice!

	ppp	*pp*	*p*	*mp*	*mf*	*f*	*ff*	*fff*
Chant	1111	2222	3333	4444	5555	6666	7777	8888

FRENCH CATHEDRALS

Traditional French Round

*   Can you sing this song so that each name is a little louder?
*   How else could you change the **dynamics**?

Or - lé - ans, Beau - gen - cy, No - tre Dame _

de Clé - ry, Ven - dô - me, Ven - dô - me.

*   Review "A Swallow Song." Plan **dynamics** for it.

MAKE MUSICAL DECISIONS

Read this poem together.
Express the ideas by the way you speak.
You will need to make several **musical decisions**.

WIND SONG

by Lilian Moore

When the wind blows
the quiet things speak.
Some whisper, some clang,
some creak.

Grasses swish.
Treetops sigh.
Flags slap
and snap at the sky.
Wires on poles
whistle and hum.
Ashcans roll.
Windows drum.

When the wind goes—
suddenly
then,
the quiet things
are quiet again.

1. Perform this poem again as a **"sound poem."**
2. Choose instruments for each idea.
3. You will still need to make the same **musical decisions**.

WILLIAM TELL OVERTURE

(excerpt)

by Gioacchino Rossini

A composer organizes **musical elements** to express an idea, describe an event, or tell a story.

- Listen to this piece of music.
- What do you think the composer is expressing?

Describe the musical decisions the composer made.

- Use the **words, musical symbols, pictures,** and **designs** shown here. Add your own.

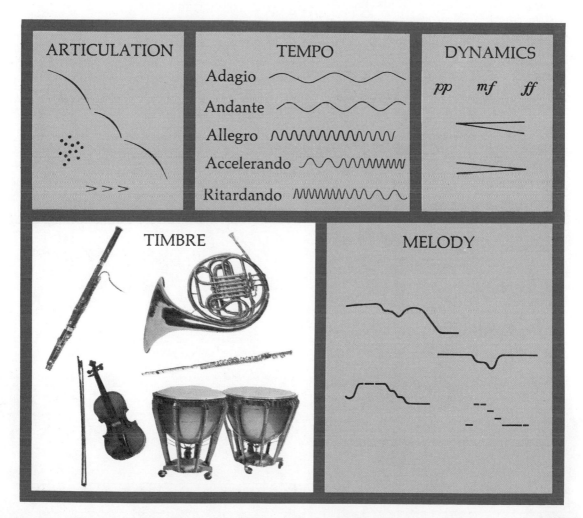

ARTICULATION

TEMPO

Adagio

Andante

Allegro

Accelerando

Ritardando

DYNAMICS

pp *mf* *ff*

TIMBRE

MELODY

VRENELI

Swiss Folk Song

Listen to this performance.
What musical decisions did these performers make about

TEMPO **DYNAMICS** **ARTICULATION**

Will you make the same decisions?

1. "O Vren - e - li, my pret- ty one, Pray tell me where's your home?"
2. "O Vren - e - li, my pret- ty one, Pray tell me where's your heart?"
3. "O Vren - e - li, my pret- ty one, Pray tell me where's your head?"

"My home it is in Swit-zer-land, It's made of wood and stone."
"O that," she said,"I gave a- way, Its pain will not de- part."
"O that, I al- so gave a- way, 'Tis with my heart,"she said.

"My home it is in Swit-zer-land, It's made of wood and stone."
"O that," she said, "I gave a - way, Its pain will not de - part."
"O that, I al - so gave a - way, 'Tis with my heart," she said.

Refrain

Yo, ho, ho, tra - la - la - la; Yo, ho, ho, tra - la - la - la;

1.
Yo, ho, ho, tra - la - la - la; Yo, ho, ho, tra - la - la - la;

2.
ho, tra - la - la - la, Yo, ho, ho.

Divide into two groups.
Group 1 sings "Yo, ho, ho."
Hold the last "ho" while **Group 2** sings "tra-la-la-la."

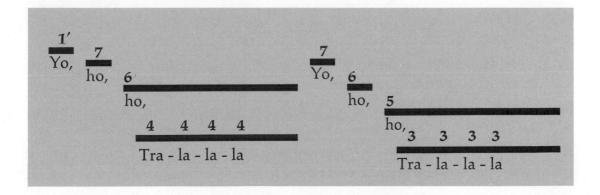

The sound of your combined voices is called a **THIRD.**

SING IN HARMONY

Sing "Lovely Evening," page 42.
Then sing it as a two-part round.
   Your voices will sound in **harmony** like this:

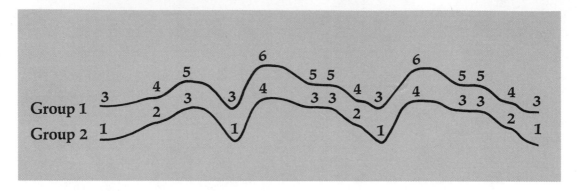

How far apart are the two groups of voices?

Sing "Where Is John," page 23.
   Sing this melody as a two-part round.
   Your voices will sound in **harmony** like this:

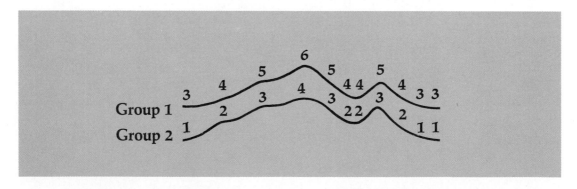

You are singing in **THIRDS**.

STREETS OF GLORY

Learn this song.
What else could you do along the streets of glory?

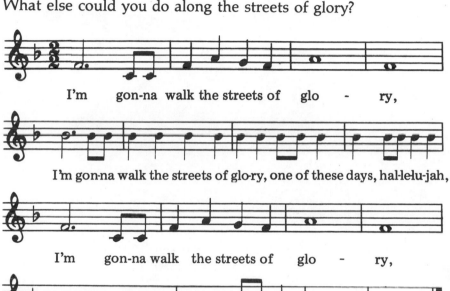

I'm gon-na walk the streets of glo - ry,

I'm gon-na walk the streets of glo-ry, one of these days, hal-le-lu-jah,

I'm gon-na walk the streets of glo - ry,

Walk the streets of glo- ry one of these days._____

You can sing this song in **THIRDS.** Divide into two groups.

Start the song together in **unison.**

Group 1 Continue to sing the melody.
Group 2 "Hop up" above the melody.

Sing a **THIRD** higher.

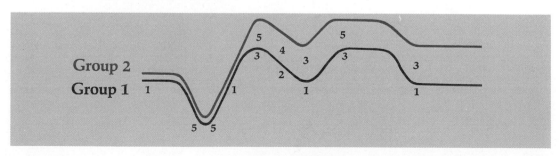

69

Check Point III

Can you . . .
- make decisions about   **tempo?**
                              articulation?
                              dynamics?

- describe the decisions
  others make about
        tempo?
    articulation?
      dynamics?

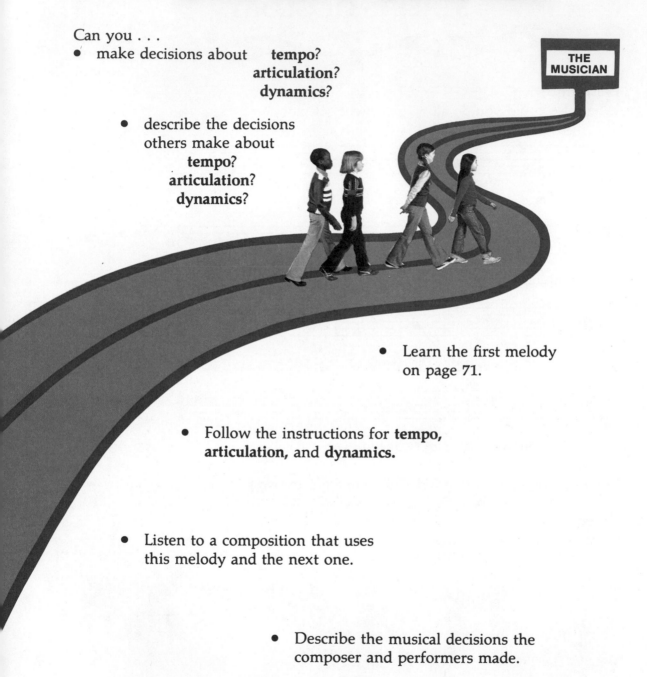

THE MUSICIAN

- Learn the first melody
  on page 71.

- Follow the instructions for **tempo,
  articulation,** and **dynamics.**

- Listen to a composition that uses
  this melody and the next one.

- Describe the musical decisions the
  composer and performers made.

SYMPHONY NO. 94 ("SURPRISE")

Second Movement

by Joseph Haydn

Andante

- Add an accompaniment to this melody.

- Use these chords:

- Now listen to this melody.

You will hear these melodies repeated many times.
- Do you hear changes in **tempo? articulation? dynamics?**
- Is anything else changed?

SOUND CATEGORIES

- How many different ways can you group these instruments?

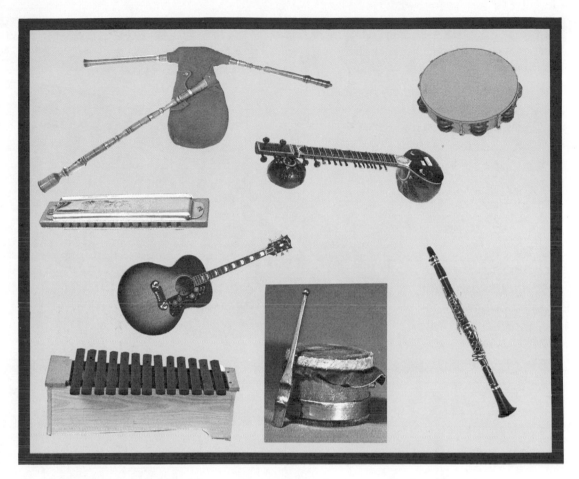

- How many ways could you group these instruments just by looking at them?
- Now listen to them! Will you group them the same way?
    Make a chart such as the one below.
    What other categories can you add?
    As you listen to each sound, mark your chart.

SOUND	Blow	Bow	? —→	Thud	Click	? —→	What else? —→
1.							
2.							
3.							
↓							

INSTRUMENTS OF THE ORCHESTRA

The instruments of the orchestra are grouped into **families.**
- Look at the pictures.
- Can you decide why they are grouped this way?

Each **family** has at least one instrument in every **range— low, middle,** and **high.**

PERCUSSION

VIOLINS

TROMBONES

FRENCH HORNS

CLARINETS

FLUTES

VIOLAS

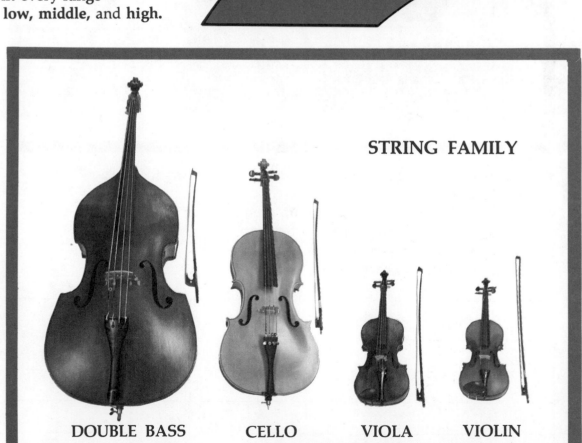

STRING FAMILY

DOUBLE BASS   CELLO   VIOLA   VIOLIN

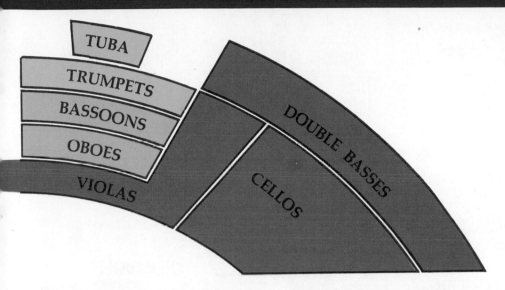

TUBA

TRUMPETS

BASSOONS

OBOES

VIOLAS

DOUBLE BASSES

CELLOS

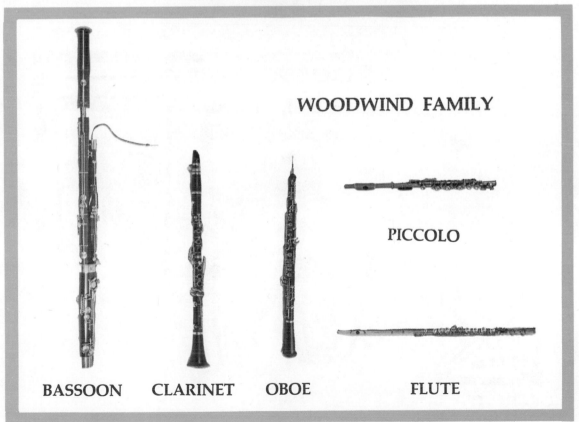

WOODWIND FAMILY

PICCOLO

BASSOON   CLARINET   OBOE   FLUTE

BRASS FAMILY

TRUMPET

FRENCH HORN

TUBA

TROMBONE

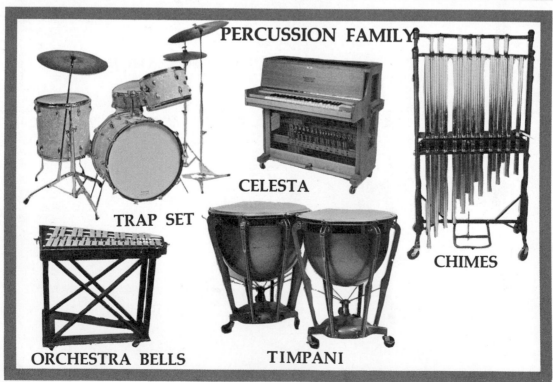

PERCUSSION FAMILY

CELESTA

CHIMES

TRAP SET

ORCHESTRA BELLS

TIMPANI

BARTÓK'S GAME OF PAIRS

Concerto for Orchestra, Second Movement

by Bela Bartók

Béla Bartók composed a **game** for different pairs of instruments in the orchestra. • Can you name each pair?

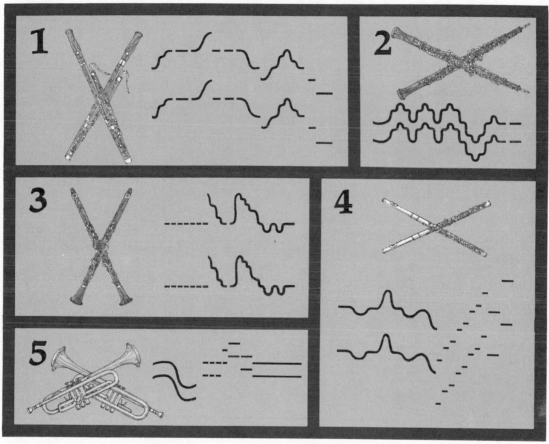

After the **game**, a **chorale** is played by brass instruments.

Then the **game** begins again. • Do you hear the same instruments?
• Do you ever hear string or percussion instruments?

THE ORCHESTRA

- Choose your favorite instrument.
- Learn its song.
- When all know their parts, sing them together.
- Can you make your voice sound like the instrument you chose?

THE INSTRUMENTS

Arranged by Julius G. Herford   Words and music by Willy Geisler

1

The vi - o - lin's ring - ing like love - ly___ sing - ing. The vi - o - lin's ring - ing like love - ly___ song.

2

The clar - i - net, the clar - i - net, makes dood-le, dood-le, dood-le, dood-le det. The clar - i - net, the clar - i - net, makes dood-le, dood-le, dood-le det.

3

The trump-et is bray-ing ta-ta-ta ta-ta-te-ta, ta-ta-ta ta-ta-te-ta. The trump-et is bray-ing ta-ta-ta ta-ta-te-ta, ta-ta-ta-ta.

4

The horn, the horn, a-wakes me at morn. The horn, the horn, a-wakes me at morn.

5

The drum's play-ing two tones and al-ways the same tones: five, one, one, five, five, five, five, five, one.

If you chose the flute, sing its song while the others hold their last pitch.

The flute's play-ing sweet-ly with tone so clear.

VOICES HAVE DIFFERENT SOUNDS

Go around the class, taking turns.
Say "Good morning" or "How are you?"
Listen carefully.
Can you group voices into categories?
Will you use the same descriptions you used for instruments?

Each of you can make your voice sound different by
changing the **quality.**
Sing this song in your natural singing voice.
Find a way to change the **quality** of your voice, and
sing the song again.

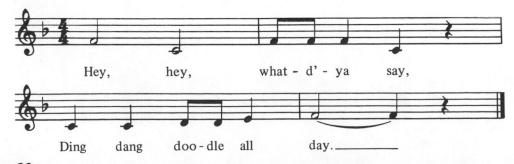

Hey,   hey,   what - d' - ya   say,

Ding   dang   doo - dle   all   day._____

ONE VOICE HAS DIFFERENT SOUNDS

Read the following drama. Use your voice to portray the different characters. How will you change the quality and pitch of your voice?

LITTLE BOY:	Father, Father, I just saw a flash, A terrible sound and a roaring crash!
FATHER:	My son, my son, imagining again. Run and play, my game's about to begin.
LITTLE BOY:	Mother! Mother! I just saw robots all over the place. I know they came from outer space.
MOTHER:	Oh, what a story! I cannot believe! Woe is me . . . you do make me grieve.
LITTLE BOY:	But Mother, oh, Mother, it's all really true. They're coming so close, what shall we do? (The door mysteriously opens.)
ROBOT:	We are here, we mean you no harm. We were forced to land on your Earthling farm.
LITTLE BOY:	What did I tell you, you see! You see!
MOTHER:	Shhhh, my son . . . I can hardly believe!
ROBOT:	We need repairs, our system is down. Do you happen to have a wire that is brown?
FATHER:	Why, yes I do. Is that all you need?
ROBOT:	That will be fine, we thank you indeed.
LITTLE BOY:	He's going away, but did you see? He was big as a mountain and fierce as could be!
FATHER:	Sometimes, my son, we really should believe you, But sometimes, you know you exaggerate, too!

THE WRAGGLE-TAGGLE GYPSIES

Old English Ballad

Act out this ballad.
- Choose someone to be the narrator.
- Who will be the lady? the gypsies? the lord? the servants?
- Can you sing with a vocal **quality** that will express the words?

1. There __ were three gyp - sies a - come to my door,
2. Then __ she pulled off her __ silk fin - ished-gown,
3. It was late last night when my lord came __ home,

And down - stairs ran this - a la - dy, O!
And put on hose of __ leath - er, O!
In - quir - ing for his __ la - dy, O!

The one sang high, and an - oth - er sang low,
The rag - ged rags a - bout __ our door,
The ser - vants said on __ ev - er - y hand,

And the oth - er sang, "Bon - ny, bon - ny Bis - cay, O!"
And she's gone __ with the wrag - gle - tag - gle gyp - sies, O!
"She's gone __ with the wrag - gle - tag - gle gyp - sies, O!"

4. Come saddle to me my milk-white steed,
   And go and seek my pony, O!
   That I may ride and seek my bride,
   Who is gone with the wraggle-taggle gypsies, O!

5. Then he rode high, and he rode low,
   He rode through wood and copses too.
   Until he came to an open field,
   And there he espied his-a lady, O!

6. "What makes you leave your house and your land?
   What makes you leave your money, O!
   What makes you leave your new-wedded lord,
   To go with the wraggle-taggle gypsies, O!"

7. "What care I for my house and my land?
   And what care I for my money, O!
   What care I for my new-wedded lord?
   I'm off with the wraggle-taggle gypsies, O!"

8. "Last night you slept in a goose-feather bed
   With the sheet turned down so bravely, O!
   But tonight you sleep in a cold, open field,
   Along with the wraggle-taggle gypsies, O!"

9. "Oh, what care I for a goose-feather bed
   With the sheet turned down so bravely, O!
   For tonight I shall sleep in a cold, open field,
   Along with the wraggle-taggle gypsies, O!"

BE A SONG LEADER

Setting the Tonality

You're on a camp-out.
Everyone wants to sing.
No one has an instrument.
Who can be the song leader and
give the **starting pitch**?

Practice giving the **starting pitch** for songs you know.
Think of a favorite song, such as "Are You Sleeping?"
- Think the melody "in your head."
- Hum a pitch you think is right for the **tonal center.**
- Everyone sing the song.
- Was the melody too high? too low?
- Try again.
- Take turns being the song leader and setting the **tonality.**

MY HAT

German Folk Song

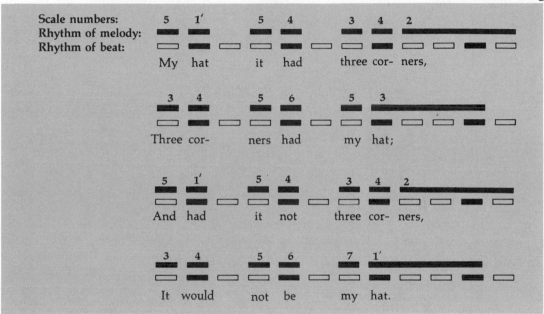

Scale numbers:	5	1'		5	4		3	4	2
Rhythm of melody:									
Rhythm of beat:									
	My	hat		it	had		three	cor-	ners,

Three cor- ners had my hat;

5 1' 5 4 3 4 2
And had it not three cor- ners,

3 4 5 6 7 1'
It would not be my hat.

Which pitches will you use? To decide—

1. Find the lowest **scale number** in the song. Find the highest.
2. Find a low pitch on the bells that is comfortable to sing.
   Find a high pitch that is comfortable to sing.
3. Will the **tonal center** be the lowest pitch?
   the highest? in between?
4. Locate the bells you will need to play the song.

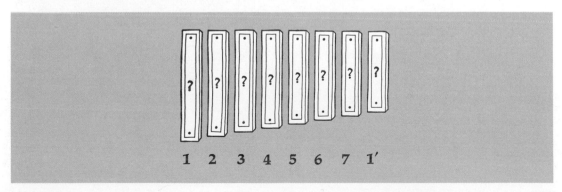

1 2 3 4 5 6 7 1'

85

Pick A Pitch

Here are two songs.
- Can you learn to play each on the resonator bells?
- Which bells will you need?

To answer that question you need to know your **"pitch facts."**
- Complete the guide sheet, **"Pitch Facts."** Then play these songs.

STARS

Words and music by Max Exner

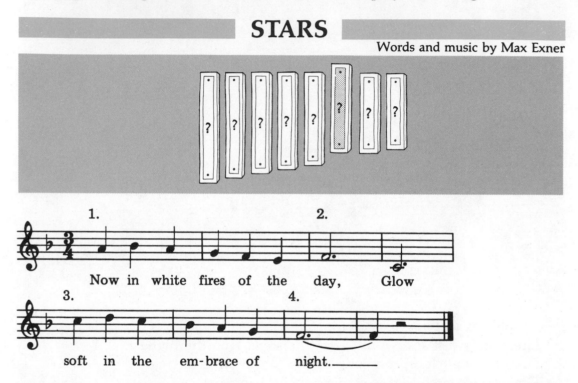

1. Now in white fires of the day, Glow
3. soft in the em-brace of night._____

LITTLE BELLS OF WESTMINSTER

Traditional Round

The lit-tle bells of West-min-ster go ding, dong, ding, dong, dong.

THE RATTLE SNA-WA-WAKE

American Folk Song

Learn this song as shown on the staff with A as the **tonal center.** Choose a different **tonal center** and sing the song again.

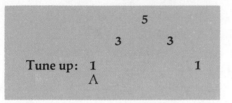

Tune up:

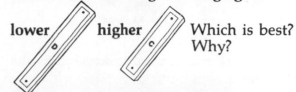

lower / **higher** / Which is best? Why?

1. A nice young ma - wa - wan Lived on the hi - wi - will;
2. He scarce had mo - wo - wowed Half round the fie - we - wield
3. "O pap - py da - wa - wad, Go tell my ga - wa - wal

A nice young ma - wa - wan, For I knew him we - we - well.
Come a rat-tle,come a sna - wa - wake And bit him on the he - we - weel.
That I'm a-goin' to di - wi - wie, For I know I sha - wa - wall."

Refrain

To my rat - tle, to my roo - rah - ree.

4. "Oh John, O Joh-wa-wahn,
Why did you go-wo-wo
Way down in the mea-we-dow
So far to mo-wo-wo?"
Refrain

5. "Oh Sal, O Sa-wa-wa-wal,
Why don't you kno-wo-wow
When the grass gets ri-wi-wipe
It must be mo-wo-wowed?"
Refrain

6. Come all young gi-gi-wirls
And shed a tea-we-wear
For this young ma-wa-wan
That died right he-we-were.
Refrain

7. Come all young me-we-wen
And warning ta-wa-wake
And don't get bi-wi-wit
By a rattle sna-wa-wake.
Refrain

87

BE A SONG LEADER II

Setting the Beat

You know how to pick a **pitch** to start a **melody**.
Can you set the **beat** to start the **rhythm**?

To set the **beat** you need to know how the **beats are grouped** in the song.

- Do they move in   **2's   3's   4's?**

"Think" the melody of "The Three Fishermen."
- Tap the **heavy** and **light beats.**
- Which picture shows your tapping pattern?

"Think" the melody of "My Hat."
- Tap the **heavy** and **light beats.**
- Which picture shows this tapping pattern?

Take turns being the song leader.
- You must show the singers the **beat.**
- Use one of these **conducting patterns.**

2's   3's   4's

- Be sure to also hum the **tonal center** and **starting pitch** to help the singers get started.

GOING STEADY
The Meter Signature

You know how the beats are grouped in "The Three Fishermen"
and "My Hat."
- Look at the first phrase of each song.
- Can you find the clue that gives this information?

THE THREE FISHERMEN

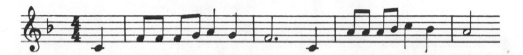

MY HAT

The clue is called the **meter signature.**
- The *top* number tells how the **beats are grouped.**
- The *bottom* number tells which **note** will
  move with the beat.

SELF-CHECK

Sing each of these songs to yourself.
Tap the **heavy** and **light beats.** How were they **grouped?**
Now look at each song. Were you right?

"Lovely Evening" (page 42)
"Who Did?" (page 33)
"Johnny" (page 37)
"When I Am Ten Years Old" (page 48)

THE UPWARD TRAIL

Traditional Words and Music

When you know this hiking song, choose someone to be the song leader. The song leader must:

- hum the **tonal center** and **starting pitch.**
- show the **meter** and **tempo** with conducting motions.

Review pages 59–61 to recall how to set a good **tempo.**

We're on the up-ward trail, we're on the up-ward trail,

Sing-ing, sing-ing, ev-ery-bod-y sing-ing, as we go.

We're on the up-ward trail, we're on the up-ward trail,

Sing-ing, sing-ing, ev-ery-bod-y sing - ing, home-ward bound.

Learn "Weggis Dance" on page 91. You can sing this song when hiking. Sing both "The Upward Trail" and "Weggis Dance" in the same **tempo.** Is that **tempo** comfortable for both songs? Why? Why not?

WEGGIS DANCE

Swiss Folk Dance

1. From Lu - cerne to ___ Weg - gis fair,
2. When we row a - cross the bay,
3. Weg - gis leads to a moun - tain high,

Hol - di - ri - di - a, hol - di - ri - a,

Shoes and stock - ings we need not wear,
There we see pret - ty maid - ens gay,
Gai - ly sing as ___ we go by,

Hol - di - ri - di - a, hol - di - a.

Refrain

Hol - di - ri - di - a, Hol - di - ri - di - a, hol - di - ri - a;

Hol - di - ri - di - a, Hol - di - ri - di - a, hol - di - a.

91

TONAL CENTER SEARCH

Divide into five groups.
- Each group takes one of the five examples of "Hop Out Of Bed."
- Follow the instructions on the Guide Sheet.

HOP OUT OF BED

Words and Music by Paul Shoner

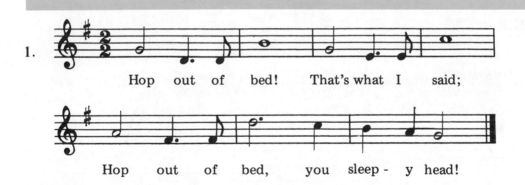

1. Hop out of bed! That's what I said;

Hop out of bed, you sleep-y head!

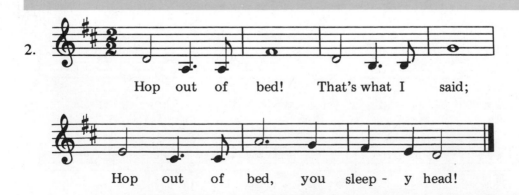

2. Hop out of bed! That's what I said;

Hop out of bed, you sleep-y head!

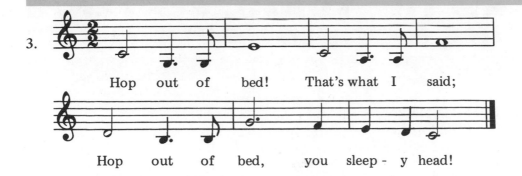

3. Hop out of bed! That's what I said;

Hop out of bed, you sleep - y head!

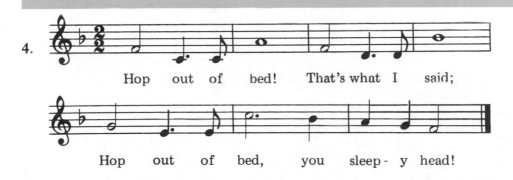

4. Hop out of bed! That's what I said;

Hop out of bed, you sleep - y head!

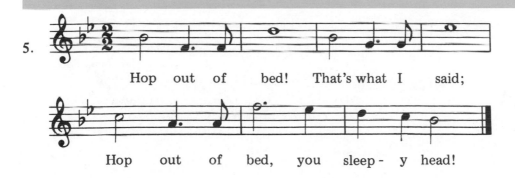

5. Hop out of bed! That's what I said;

Hop out of bed, you sleep - y head!

Listen to each group sing "Hop Out Of Bed."
- What difference do you *hear?* Is anything the same?

Compare your answers on the Guide Sheets.
- What differences do you *find?* Is anything the same?

Compare the five examples of "Hop Out Of Bed" in your book.
- What differences do you *see?* Is anything the same?

Is there a clue to help you discover that each example
has a different **tonal center**?

FIND THE TONAL CENTER: THE KEY SIGNATURE— SHARPS

Look at each **key signature.**
Count up from the **tonal center** to the last **sharp.**
What do you discover? Can you make a rule?

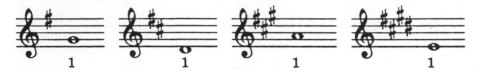

BANANA BOAT LOADER'S SONG

Jamaican Folk Song

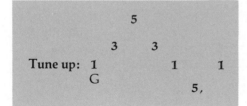

Tune up:

What is the **tonal center** of this song?
Set the **tonality.**
Play the I chord on the autoharp.

Sing the melody with scale numbers.

Day oh! Day_ oh! Day is break - ing,_ I wan' go home. _

1. Come, Mis - ter Tal - ly - man, come tal - ly my ba - nan - as.
2. Came here for work, I did - n't come here for to i - dle.

94

Day is break - ing, __ I wan' go home. __

3. Three han', four han', five han', Bunch!

Six han', seven han', eight han', Bunch!

Day is break - ing, __ I wan' go home. __

4. So check them, and check them, but check with cau - tion.
5. My back is a - break - ing with bare ex - haus - tion.
6. Don't give me all the bunch-es, I'm no horse with bri - dle.

4-5. | 6.

Day is break - ing, __ I wan' go home, __ wan' go home, __

FIND THE TONAL CENTER: THE KEY SIGNATURE— FLATS

Look at each **key signature** using **flats.**
Count up from "1" to the last **flat.**
Can you make a rule?

ROCKA MY SOUL

Spiritual

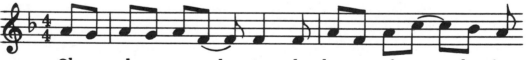

Oh, a rock-a my soul __ in the bos-om of A - bra-ham,

A rock-a my soul __ in the bos-om of A - bra-ham,

A rock-a my soul __ in the bos-om of A - bra-ham,

Oh, rock-a my soul.

So high, you can't get o-ver it;

So low, you can't get un-der it;

So wide, you can't get a-round it;

You must go in at the door.

Partners

- Sing this song in a special way.
    Divide into two groups.
    Group 1 sings the first two phrases, while
    Group 2 sings the last two phrases.
- Continue to sing. This time
    Group 1 will be singing the last two phrases, while
    Group 2 sings the first two phrases.

- Listen to the **harmony** created when the two melodies
are sounded together.

FANFARE FOR ST. EDMUNDSBURY

by Benjamin Britten

You have been singing partner songs. This is a "triplet" song. Listen to each trumpet play its melody. Follow the notation that is shown below.

When you have listened carefully to each solo part, listen to the three trumpets combine their melodies.

- Can you follow each trumpet's melody?

PLANTING RICE

Philippine Folk Song

Tune up:

```
              5
        3        3
      1            1
      C
```

With spirit

C   C   C

Plant-ing rice is nev - er fun, Work from morn till set of

G7   G7   G7

sun, Can - not sit and can - not stand, Plant the

G7   C   Refrain   C

seed - lings all by hand. Plant - ing rice is no

C   C   G7

fun, Work from morn till set of sun, Can - not

G7   G7   G7   C

sit, can - not stand, Plant the seed - lings all by hand.

- Accompany "Planting Rice" on the autoharp.
  You will use two chords: [C] [G7] When will you change?
                I   V7

  You can sing the **verse** and **refrain** together as "partners."
- Why will it sound all right?

BARN YARD BEDLAM

- Learn "Old Gray Mare" and "The Sow Got the Measles."
- Then divide into two groups.
    Group 1 sings the verse of "Old Gray Mare."
    Group 2 sings "The Sow Got the Measles."

OLD GRAY MARE

Traditional

Oh, the old gray mare, she ain't what she used to be,

Ain't what she used to be, ain't what she used to be.

The old gray mare she ain't what she used to be,

Man - y long years a - go.

Man - y long years a - go,

man - y long years a - go.

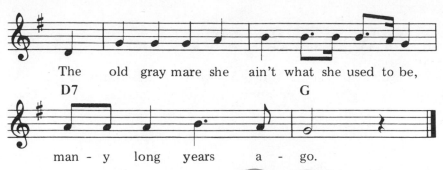

The old gray mare she ain't what she used to be,

man-y long years a-go.

THE SOW GOT THE MEASLES

Traditional

1. How do you think I start-ed in life? I
2. What do you think I did with her hide?
3. What do you think I did with her tail?

got me a sow and oth-er such things.
Made the best sad-dle you ev-er did ride,
Made me a whip and al-so a flail,

Pig or hog or some such thing, The
Saddle or bridle or some such thing, The
Whip or whip-handle some such thing, The

sow got the meas-les and she died in the spring.
sow got the meas-les and she died in the spring.
sow got the meas-les and she died in the spring.

Add to the bedlam!
- A third group sings "Mary Had A Little Lamb."
- A fourth group sings "Go Tell Aunt Rhodie."

Your Own Partner Song

Make up your own partner song to add to the "Barn Yard Bedlam."
Use these words, or make up your own about another animal.

| The | poor | old | cow | says | "moo" |

| 'Cause | she | has | noth - ing | to | do. |

| And | all | she can say, | | all | through the day |

| Is | "moo," | "moo," | "moo," | "moo," | "moo." |

Plan your melody.
- Look at the chords for "Old Gray Mare."
- Write down the name of the chord for each measure.
- Use any of these pitches for measures
  that are accompanied
  by the **I (G)** chord:

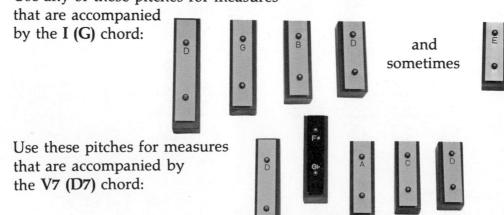

and
sometimes

- Use these pitches for measures
  that are accompanied by
  the **V7 (D7)** chord:

102

Check Point IV

Can you . . .
- find the **tonal center**?
- sing a melody with **scale numbers**?
- play a melody on an instrument?
- hear the **tonal center**? set it?

THE MUSICIAN

Can you . . .
- hear **phrase** endings?
- describe **same** and **different** sections?

Can you . . .
- identify instruments?
- perform using different vocal **qualities**?

Can you . . .
- make musical decisions about
  tempo?
  articulation?
  dynamics?

Can you . . .
- hear **meter**? set the **meter**?
- perform **rhythms** in relation to the shortest sound?
- describe **rhythms** you hear?

Can you . . .
- perform **ostinati**?
  partner songs?
  accompaniments?
- hear chord changes?

Can you . . .
- do all of these things as you learn "The 59th Street Bridge Song" on page 104?

THE 59TH STREET BRIDGE SONG

Words and music by Paul Simon

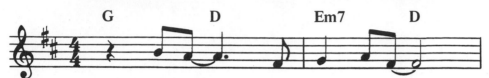

Slow down,— you move too fast.—

You got to make the morn - ing last.— Just

kick - in' down the cob-ble stones,—

look-in' for fun and feel - in' groov-y. _____

Hel-lo lamp-post, what-cha know-in',

I've come to watch your flow - ers grow - in'.

Ain't 'cha got no rhymes___ for me?

Doot-in' doo-doo, feel-in' groov-y. _____ Got

no deeds to do, no prom - i - ses to keep. I'm

dap-pled and drow-sy and read - y to sleep. Let the

morn - ing - time drop all its pet-als on me.

Life, I love you, All is groov - y._____

You learned the song "Happiness Runs" on page 2.
You can perform it as an **ostinato** accompaniment to "The 59th
Street Bridge Song."
Can you also make up an **ostinato** for this song?

THE LITTLE TRAIN OF THE CAIPIRA

by Heitor Villa-Lobos

Follow the call numbers as you listen.

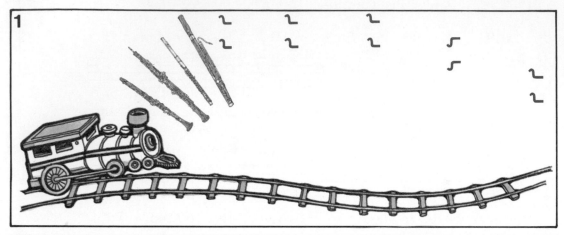

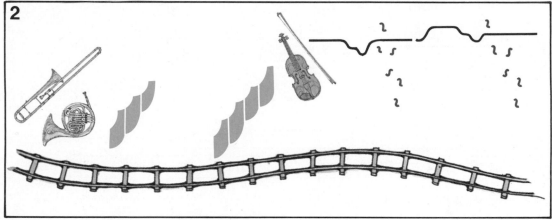

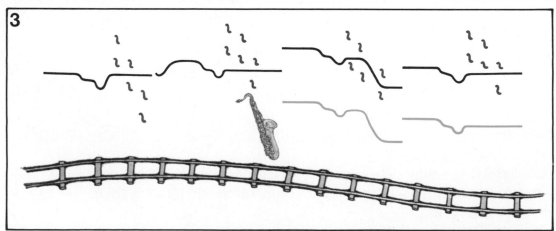

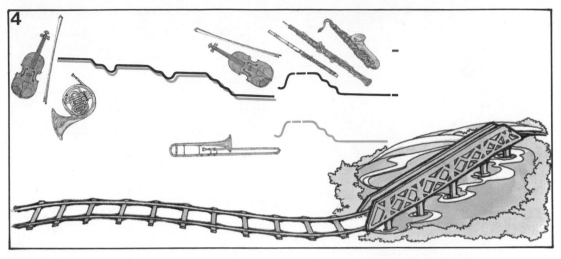

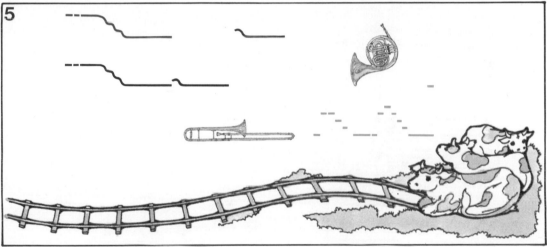

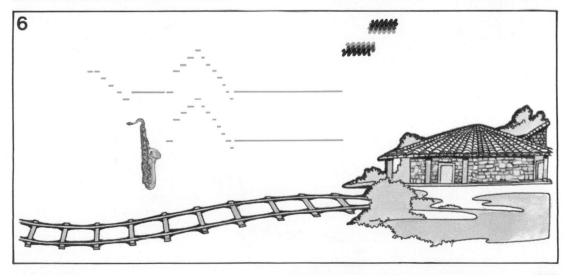

7

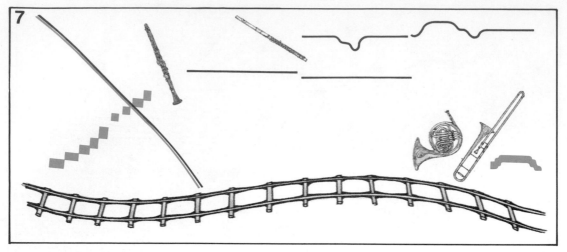

8

9

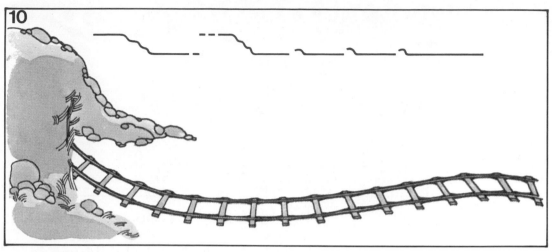

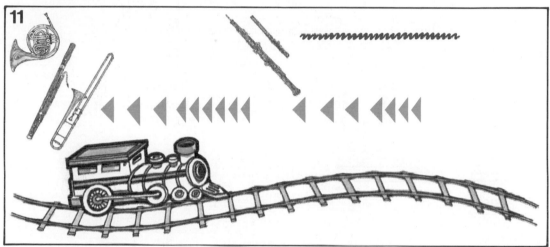

● Listen to another performance. What differences do you notice?

THE CUCKOO

Austrian Folk Song

1. O I went to Pe - ter's flow - ing spring Where the
2. Af - ter Eas - ter come __ sun - ny days That will
3. When I've mar - ried my __ maid - en fair, What then

wa - ter's so good, And I heard there the
melt all the snow; Then I'll mar - ry my
can I de - sire? O a home for her

cuck - oo As she called from the wood.
maid - en fair, We'll be hap - py, I know.
tend - ing And some wood for the fire.

Refrain

Ho - li - ah, Ho - le - rah - hi - hi - ah, Ho - le - rah cuck - oo!

Ho - le - rah - hi - hi - ah, Ho - le - rah cuck - oo! Ho - le - rah - hi - hi - ah,

Ho - le - rah cuck - oo! Ho - le - rah - hi - hi - ah - ho!

Here are some accompaniment patterns for "The Cuckoo."
- Will you perform all of them at the same time?
  How will you decide?
- Might you use some for the **verse,** others for the **refrain**?

Arranged by Sharon Falk

Soprano Xylophone

1.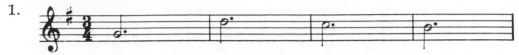

Alto Xylophone

2.

Bass Xylophone

3.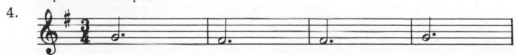

G   D   D   E   F♯   G

Soprano Metallophone

4.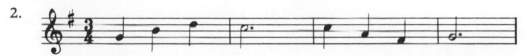

Alto Metallophone

5.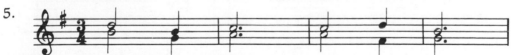

Alto Glockenspiel

6.

SWING LOW, SWEET CHARIOT

Spiritual
Arranged by William S. Haynie

Swing low, sweet char - i - ot, ___ Com-ing for to car - ry me home,

Swing low, sweet char - i - ot, ___ Com- ing for to car- ry me home.

1. I looked o - ver Jor - dan and what did I see? ___
2. If you get ___ there ___ be - fore ___ I do, ___
3. I'm some - times ___ up ___ and some - times down, ___

A band ___ of an - gels
Just tell ___ my friends I'm
But still ___ my soul feels

Com - ing for to car - ry me home.

MORE MUSIC TO EXPLORE

Be A Performer

THE PERFORMER

SING ALONE . . . SING TOGETHER . . .

PLAY ALONE . . . PLAY TOGETHER . . .

WE SING OF GOLDEN MORNINGS

Words Adapted by Vincent Silliman
from a poem by Ralph Waldo Emerson

Music from William Walker's
Southern Harmony

Brightly

1. We sing of gold-en morn - ings, We sing of spar- kling seas,
2. We sing the heart cou - ra - geous, The youth- ful, ea - ger mind;

Of prai- ries, val - leys, moun-tains, And state - ly for - est trees.
We sing of hopes un -daunt - ed, Of friend - ly ways and kind.

We sing of flash-ing sun - shine And life - be -stow-ing rain,
We sing the ros- es wait - ing Be -neath the deep-piled snow;

Of birds a - mong the branch- es, And spring-time come a - gain.
We sing, when night is dark - est, The day's re - turn- ing glow.

YELLOW SUBMARINE

Words and Music
by John Lennon and Paul McCartney

Can you tap this **uneven rhythm** as you listen?

Why will this song be easy to learn?

March tempo

In the town _____ where I was born lived a

man _____ who sailed to sea, And he told _____ us of his

life in the land _____ of sub - ma -

rines. So we sailed _____ up to the sun till we

found _____ the sea of green. And we lived _____ be- neath the

waves in our yel - low sub - ma - rine.

Chorus

We all live in a yel - low sub - ma - rine,

yel - low sub - ma - rine, yel - low sub - ma - rine,

We all live in a yel - low sub - ma - rine,

yel - low sub - ma - rine, yel - low sub - ma - rine. { And our
                                                     { As we

friends __ are all on board, man - y more of them __ live next
live __ a life of ease, ev - ery one of us __ has all we

1.
door. And the band __ be - gins to play . . .
need: Sky of blue __ and sea of

2.   *Repeat Chorus from the 𝄋 and fade.*
green, in our yel - low sub - ma - rine.

THIS TRAIN

American Folk Song

Listen to the recording.
Tap short sounds as you listen.
The melody usually moves with this short sound.

Can you find a place in the song where the rhythm moves with
even shorter sounds?

Add an accompaniment based
on this **shortest sound.**

1. This train   is bound for glo - ry, This train,__
2. This train   don't pull no ex - tras, This train,__

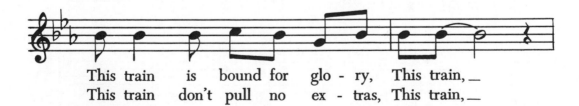

This train   is bound for glo - ry, This train,__
This train   don't pull no ex - tras, This train,__

This   train   is   bound for   glo - ry,
This   train   don't   pull   no   ex - tras,

118

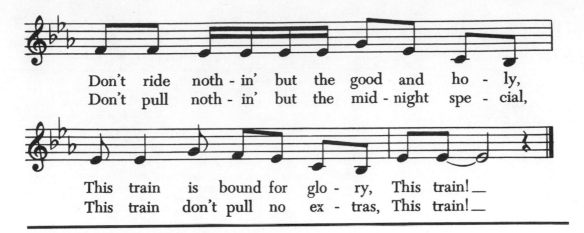

Don't ride noth-in' but the good and ho - ly,
Don't pull noth-in' but the mid-night spe - cial,

This train is bound for glo - ry, This train! ___
This train don't pull no ex - tras, This train! ___

Perform your own accompaniment on piano.

- Play this pattern   **OR**   this pattern.

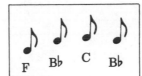

- Find the pitches you will need:

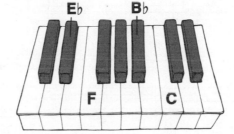

Can you decide when you will need to change from the first pattern to the second? When will you go back to the first?

- Someone else may add a whistle sound. Find your pitches:

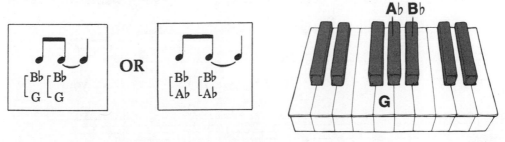

When will you play the whistle sound?

ROCK ISLAND LINE

Work Song

Perform this accompaniment:

Chant ch ch ch ch ch ch ch ch

With a steady beat

I say the Rock Is - land Line ___ is a

might - y good road, ___ I say the Rock Is - land Line ___

___ is the road to ride; Oh, the Rock Is - land Line ___

___ is a might - y good road, ___ If you want to

ride it, got to ride it like you're fly - in'; Buy your

tick - et at the sta - tion on the Rock Is - land Line.

THE SHANTY BOYS IN THE PINE

Lumberjack Song

- Describe each note in relation to the **shortest sound.**

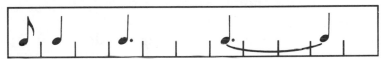

- Learn the rhythm of the song.

1. Come all ye jol - ly shan - ty boys, come lis - ten to my song; —
2. The chop - pers and the saw - yers, they lay the tim - ber low, —
3. The bro - ken ice is float - ing, and sun - ny is the sky; —

It's all a - bout the shan - ties and how they get a - long. —
The skid - ders and the swamp - ers, they hol - ler to and fro, —
Three hun - dred big and strong men are want - ed on the drive. —

They are a jol - ly crew of boys, so mer - ry and so fine, —
And then there come the load - ers, be - fore the break of day; —
With cant hooks and with jam - pikes these no - ble men do go, —

Who while a - way the win - ters a - cut - ting down the pine. —
Come load — up the teams, boys, and to the woods a - way. —
And risk their lives each spring - time on some big stream you know. —

121

DAKOTA HYMN

Words paraphrased by William Frazier

American Indian Melody

Which note represents the **shortest sound**?
Which note is the **beat note**?
Look at page 124. On which **scale** is this song based?

1. Man - y   and   great,   O   God,   are   thy   things,
2. Grant un - to   us   com - mun - ion   with   thee,

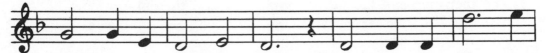

Mak - er   of   earth and   sky.   Thy hands have set   the
Thou star - a - bid - ing   one;   Come un - to   us   and

heav - ens   with   stars,   Thy   fin - gers   spread   the
dwell   with ___ us;   With   thee   are   found   the

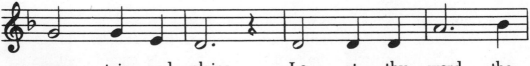

moun - tains   and   plains.   Lo,   at   thy   word   the
gifts   of ___ life.   Bless   us   with   life   that

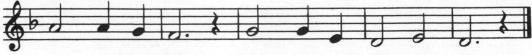

wa - ters were formed;   Deep   seas o - bey   thy   voice.
has   no ___ end,   E - ter - nal   life   with   thee.

122

MARY ANN

Words by Kathy Alexander   Calypso Song

- Find this **syncopated rhythm** in the song.

- Draw the rhythm of the whole song with your "rhythm ruler."

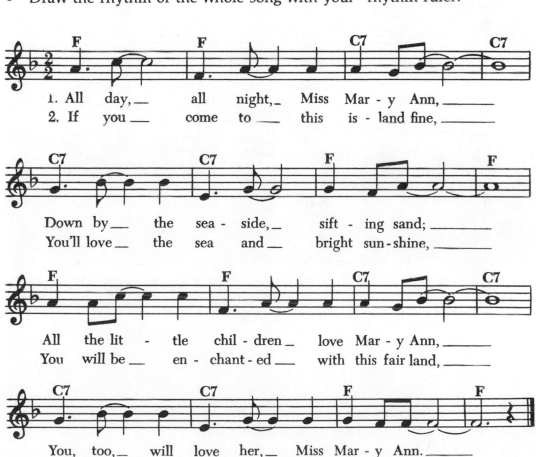

1. All day, __ all night, __ Miss Mar - y Ann, _____
2. If you __ come to __ this is - land fine, _____

Down by __ the sea - side, __ sift - ing sand; _____
You'll love __ the sea and __ bright sun - shine, _____

All the lit - tle chil - dren __ love Mar - y Ann, _____
You will be __ en - chant - ed __ with this fair land, _____

You, too, __ will love her, __ Miss Mar - y Ann. _____
You'll be __ be - witched by __ Miss Mar - y Ann. _____

ALLELUJAH, AMEN

Traditional

Tune up:
1   3   5   1'

- Sing the song with **scale numbers.**

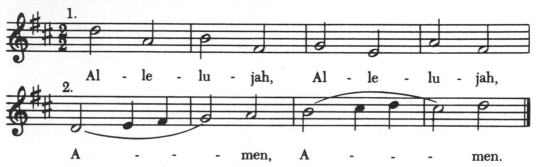

Al - le - lu - jah,   Al - le - lu - jah,

A - - - men,   A - - - men.

On which of these **scales** is the melody based?

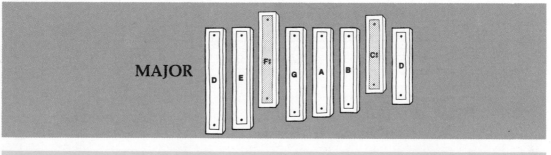

Play the melody using the bells of the correct **scale.**
Play the melody again using the bells of the other **scale.**

- What has happened to the sound?

124

COME TO THE LAND

Israeli Folk Song

Play the two **scales** shown on page 124 again.
On which of these **scales** is "Come to the Land" based?
How can you decide?

Come to the land with joy and with spir - it,

Come to our na - tive land; We have plowed the

fields and have plant-ed grain, We'll reap a might - y har - vest.

Play the melody using the bells of the correct **scale**.
Play the melody using the bells of the other **scale**.
- What has happened to the sound?

A LA NANITA NANA

English Words Adapted   Spanish Folk Melody

In this song the **tonal center** is always the **same**.
There is something that is sometimes **different**.
Listen to the recording. Can you decide what changes?

A la na - ni - ta na - na, na - ni - ta
e - a, na - ni - ta e - a,
An - gels your watch are keep - ing, will hush your
weep - ing, bring peace - ful sleep - ing.
The night - in - gale is sing - ing, foun - tain is play - ing,

Your lit - tle cra - dle swing-ing in bran-ches sway - ing.

A la na - ni - ta na - na, na - ni - ta e - a.

A la na - ni - ta na - na, na - ni - ta e - a.

When you know the melody well, turn to the next page.
Add an accompaniment.

• How will you know when to play each pattern?

Accompany "A La Nanita Nana"

- Choose a **conductor**.
- Choose three accompanists.
- Choose a group of singers.

What musical decisions must the **conductor** make?
Review pages 58–64 to be sure you are correct.

Soprano Glockenspiel

Alto Metallophone

Bass Xylophone

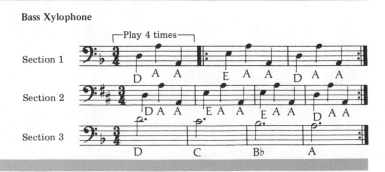

THE CONDUCTOR

Choose this song or one on page 130 or 132.
As the **conductor,** you must make several musical decisions.

TEMPO ARTICULATION DYNAMICS

- How will you tell your performers . . .

    how to **start?**
    how to **stop?**

The discussion on pages 84 and 88 will help you decide.

LULLABY ROUND

Traditional Round

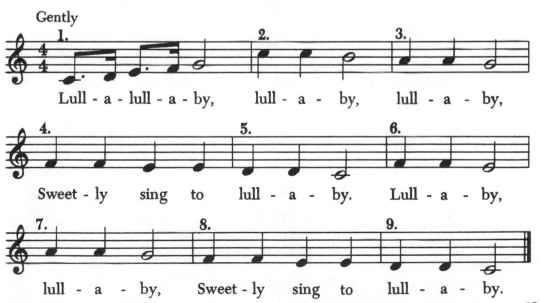

Gently

Lull - a - lull - a - by,   lull - a - by,   lull - a - by,

Sweet - ly   sing   to   lull - a - by.   Lull - a - by,

lull - a - by,   Sweet - ly   sing   to   lull - a - by.

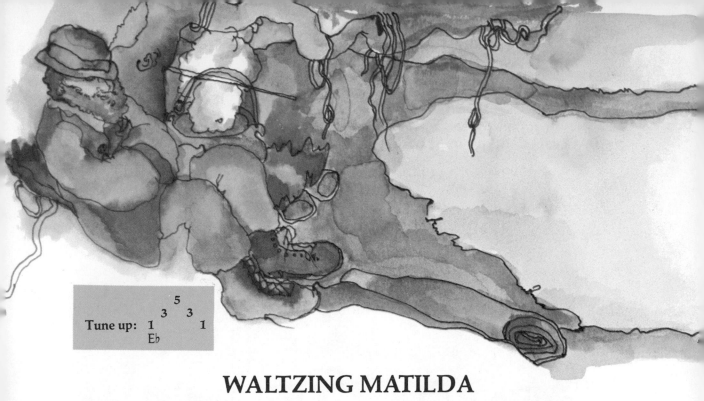

Tune up:
```
        5
      3   3
  1         1
  Eb
```

WALTZING MATILDA

Words by A.B. Patterson

Music by Marie Cowan

1. Once a jol - ly swag - man camped by a bil - la - bong,
2. Down came a jum - buck to drink at the bil - la - bong,

Un - der the shade of a coo - li - bah tree,
Up jumped the swag - man, grabbed him with glee,

And he sang as he sat and wait - ed while his bil - ly boiled:)
And he sang as he shoved that jum - buck in his tuck - er - bag:)

Fine

"You'll come a - waltz - ing, Ma - til - da, with me."

130

"Waltz - ing Ma - til - da, waltz - ing Ma - til - da,

D.S. al Fine

You'll come a - waltz - ing, Ma - til - da, with me."

3. Down came the squatter mounted on his thorobred,
Up came the troopers, one, two, three,
"Who's that jolly jumbuck you've got in your tucker-bag?
You'll come a-waltzing, Matilda, with me."
"Waltzing Matilda, waltzing Matilda,
You'll come a-waltzing, Matilda, with me."
"Who's that jolly jumbuck you've got in your tucker-bag?
You'll come a-waltzing, Matilda, with me."

4. Up jumped the swagman, sprang into the billabong,
"You'll never catch me alive!" said he.
And his ghost may be heard as you pass by the billabong:
"You'll come a-waltzing, Matilda, with me."
"Waltzing Matilda, waltzing Matilda,
You'll come a-waltzing, Matilda, with me."
And his ghost may be heard as you pass by that billabong:
"You'll come a-waltzing, Matilda, with me."

I'M LOOKING OVER A FOUR LEAF CLOVER

Words by Mort Dixon   Music by Harry Woods

- Locate the shortest sound in the song.
- Locate the sound that will move with the beat.
- Tap the beat. Chant the words.
- Can you find places where the accent of the words comes **before** the accent of the beat, making a **syncopated** rhythm?

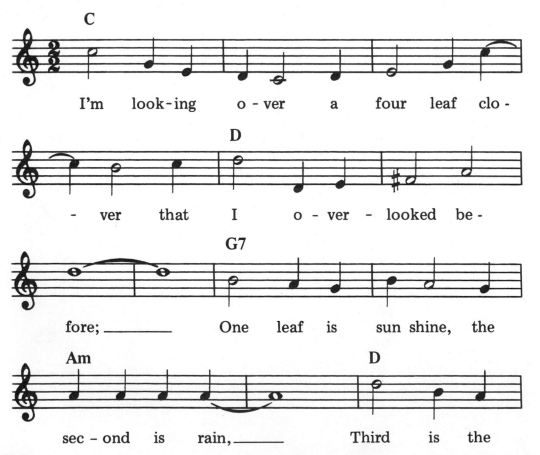

132

ros - es   that   grow   in   the   lane,_____

No   need   ex - plain - ing,   the   one   re - main -

- ing   is   some - bod - y   I   a -

dore._____   I'm   look - ing

o - ver   a   four   leaf   clo - ver   that

I   o - ver - looked   be - fore.

MY LORD, WHAT A MORNING

Spiritual

My Lord, what a morn-ing, My Lord, what a morn-ing,

Fine

My Lord, what a morn-ing, When the stars be-gin to fall.

1. You'll hear the trum-pet sound
2. You'll hear the sin-ners mourn } To wake the na-tions un-der-ground,
3. You'll hear the Chris-tians shout

D.C. al Fine

Look-ing to my God's right hand, When the stars be-gin to fall.

134

ZUM GALI GALI

Israeli Work Song

- Sing the chant softly as an **introduction** to the song.
- At the end of the fourth verse, repeat the chant several times as a **coda.**
- Let your voices grow gradually softer in a **diminuendo.**
- Gradually sing more slowly during the last repetition as a **ritardando.**

(Melody)

1. He - cha - lutz   l' - maan a - vo - dah; _____
2. A - vo - dah   l' - maan he - cha - lutz; _____
3. He - cha - lutz   l' - maan ha - b'tu - lah; _____
4. Ha - sha - lom   l' - maan ha - 'a - mim; _____

Chant

Zum ga - li ga - li ga - li, Zum ga - li ga - li,

___ A - vo - dah   l' - maan he - cha - lutz.
___ He - cha - lutz   l' - maan a - vo - dah.
___ Ha - b'tu - lah   l' - maan he - cha - lutz.
___ Ha - 'a - mim   l' - maan ha - sha - lom.

Zum ga - li ga - li ga - li, Zum ga - li ga - li.

135

KOOKABURRA

Australian Round

The **conductor** should decide . . .
- when the singers will perform in **unison.**
- when they will sing as a **round.**
- which **accompaniment patterns** to use.

1. Kook - a - bur - ra sits in the old gum tree;___
2. Kook - a - bur - ra sits in the old gum tree, ___

Mer - ry mer - ry king of the bush is he. ___
Eat - ing all the gum drops ___ he can see. ___

Laugh, kook - a - bur - ra, laugh, kook - a - bur - ra,
Laugh, kook - a - bur - ra, laugh, kook - a - bur - ra,

Gay your life must be. _____
Leave some there for me. _____

Arranged by Sharon Falk

Soprano Glockenspiel

1.

Alto Glockenspiel

2.

Soprano Xylophone

3.

Alto Xylophone I

4.

Alto Xylophone II

5.

Alto Metallophone

6.

Bass Xylophone

7.

D   A   B   G   D   A   B   A

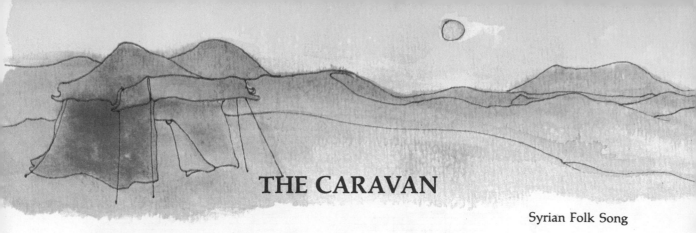

THE CARAVAN

Syrian Folk Song

Group 1 sings the **melody** while **Group 2** sings an **ostinato**.

Tramp, tramp, heav-y go the cam - els, Tramp, tramp,

Tramp, tramp, heav - y, Tramp, tramp,

cam - els heav-y lad - en, Swing - ing, sway - ing,

heav - y, Swing - ing,

on the road to Bagh - dad, Heav-y goes the car - a van.

sway - ing, Heav - y bur - den.

Heav - y goes the car - a - van.

Car - a - van.

Add an accompaniment:

(Play 4 times)

High-pitched drum:

(Play 4 times)

Finger cymbals:

Bass Metallophone:

B
E

KUM BA YAH

African Folk Song

This song comes from Africa.
People everywhere enjoy singing it.
- Can someone play the accompaniment on the autoharp
  to help the class learn the melody?

2. Someone's crying, Lord . . .
3. Someone's singing, Lord . . .
4. Someone's praying, Lord . . .

Divide into two groups. Follow the arrows:

- You sang in **UNISON** ➞ You sang in **THIRDS** ⇉
- Sing "Kum Ba Yah" in **unison** and **thirds**.

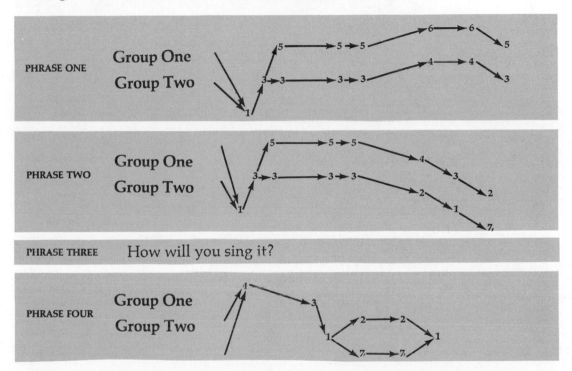

PHRASE ONE   Group One / Group Two

PHRASE TWO   Group One / Group Two

PHRASE THREE   How will you sing it?

PHRASE FOUR   Group One / Group Two

- When you can sing well in **THIRDS,** try adding another part!

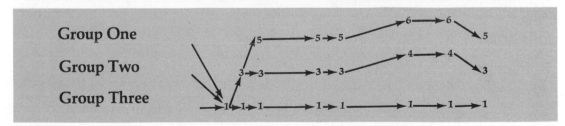

Group One

Group Two

Group Three

- There are two places where Group 3 needs to change to 7, and then back to 1:

Can you hear where these places are?

MARCHING TO PRETORIA

South African Folk Melody   Words by Josef Marais

- You can sing in **thirds** following **scale numbers:**

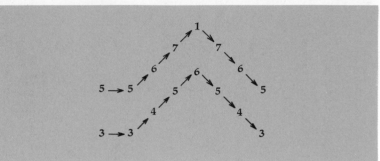

- Can you sing in **thirds** following **notes**?

Where will you sing "Marching to Pretoria" in **thirds**?

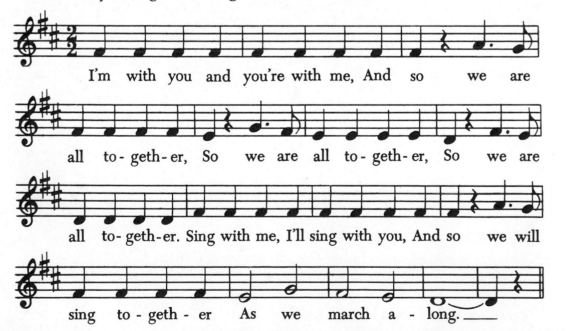

I'm with you and you're with me, And so we are

all to-geth-er, So we are all to-geth-er, So we are

all to-geth-er. Sing with me, I'll sing with you, And so we will

sing to-geth-er As we march a-long. ____

142

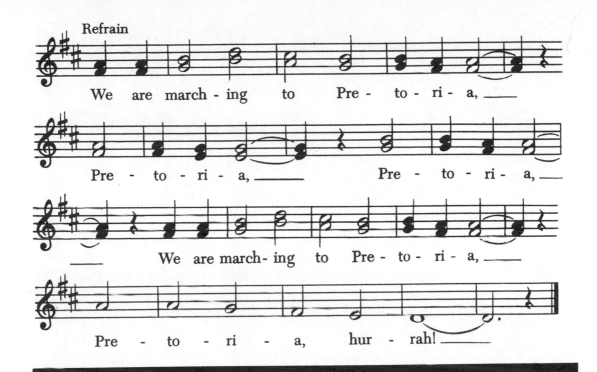

Refrain

We are march-ing to Pre - to - ri - a, ___

Pre - to - ri - a, ___ Pre - to - ri - a, ___

___ We are march-ing to Pre - to - ri - a, ___

Pre - to - ri - a, hur - rah! ___

Play a "marching" accompaniment on the piano or bells:

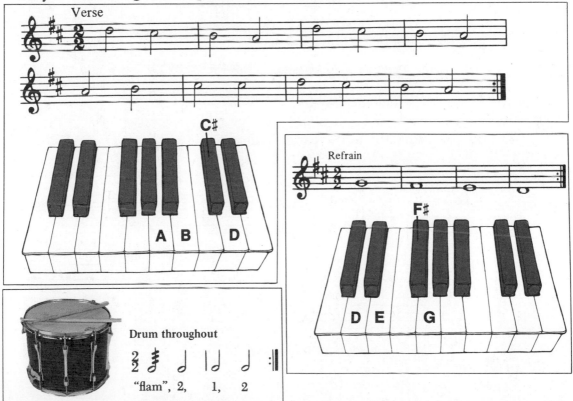

Verse

Refrain

Drum throughout

"flam", 2, 1, 2

FOLLOW ME

Traditional Carol

- Learn this hand drum rhythm.
- Then work in pairs and play it as a **canon.**
  The **leader** begins.
  The **follower** always plays two beats later.

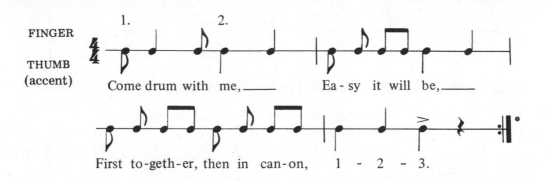

FINGER

THUMB
(accent)

Come drum with me,_____ Ea - sy it will be,_____

First to-geth-er, then in can-on, 1 - 2 - 3.

- Learn to sing this melodic **canon.**
- Why is "Follow Me" a good title?
- What do you think the term **"canon"** means?

Come a - long, Sing a song,

Come a - long, Sing a

*From *Series III, Music With Children* by Grace C. Nash.
Used by permission.

Fol - low me; It is eas - y, you can

song, Fol - low me; It is

see. Ev - ery day, In this way,

eas - y, you can see. Ev - ery day, In this

Just re - peat 'Til the tune's com - plete.

way, Just re - peat, com - plete._____

MAKE UP YOUR OWN PERCUSSION CANON

- **Performer 1** Play a pattern on any instrument you choose.
- **Performer 2** Echo **Performer 1's** pattern on another instrument.
- **Performer 1** may begin another pattern before **Performer 2** has completed the echo!
- **Performer 2** must listen carefully to be sure to repeat exactly what **Performer 1** has played!

JINGLE, JANGLE, JINGLE

Words by Frank Loesser

Music by Joseph J. Lilley

- When does this two-part song sound like a **round**?
- When does it sound in **thirds**?
- When will you sing in **unison**?

Refrain

I got spurs that jin - gle, jan - gle, jin - gle, _____

I got spurs that

_____ As I go rid - in' mer - ri - ly a - long. _____

jin - gle, jan - gle, jin - gle, _____ As I go rid - in'

HOW DOES MY LADY'S GARDEN GROW?

Words from Mother Goose

Music by Arthur Frackenpohl

This song is a **round.**

- How can you tell by looking at the music?

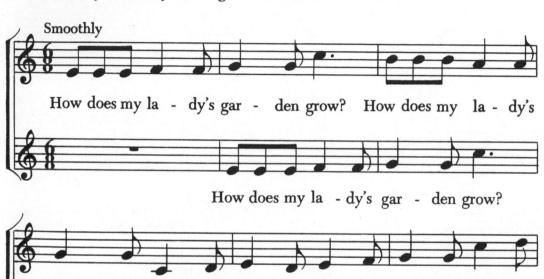

Smoothly

How does my la - dy's gar - den grow? How does my la - dy's

How does my la - dy's gar - den grow?

gar - den grow? With sil - ver bells and cock - le - shells, And

How does my la - dy's gar - den grow? With sil - ver bells and

pret - ty maids all in a row.

cock - le - shells, And pret - ty maids all in a row.

148

LEARN TO PLAY THE AUTOHARP

It's as easy as "one, two, three!"

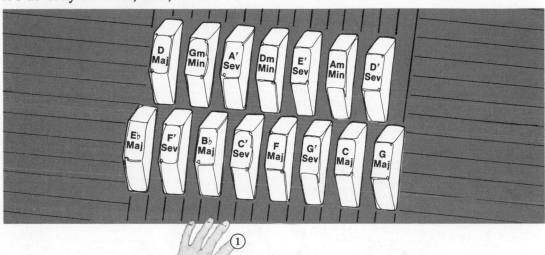

Easy as "one . . ."

- Play an expressive accompaniment as you speak these words.
- Use only:

THE WIND

by B.A.

Wind through my window,
Wind through my door,
Wind whirls 'round my feet,
Low on the floor.

Wind up the chimney,
Away in the sky,
Ruffling the bird wings
As it swishes by.

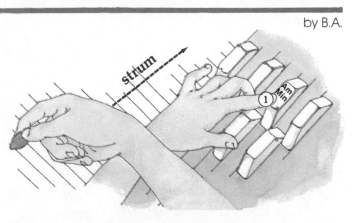

- Find the chord button.

Press it down firmly with your left index finger.
- Use your right hand to strum the chord while you sing.

THREE BLIND MICE

Traditional Round

Three blind mice,— three blind mice,— See how they run,—

see how they run!— They all ran af-ter the farm-er's wife, She

cut off their tails with a carv - ing knife; Did ev - er you see such a

sight in your life As three blind mice?

Sing "Three Blind Mice" several times.
Each time, choose a different **major** chord and change the beginning pitch of the melody.

PLAY:

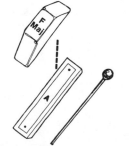
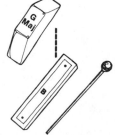

BEGIN SINGING:

What was different about your singing when you repeated the round in each of the **major keys**?
- Which was your best **key** for singing?

- Sing and accompany "Hey, Ho! Anybody Home?" page 54.

- Use one **minor** chord: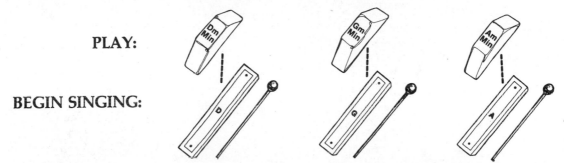

- Repeat the song in different **minor keys,** changing the first pitch.

PLAY:

BEGIN SINGING:

- Which was your best **key** for singing?

CHICKA-HANKA

Track Laborer's Song

- Accompany this song with one **minor** chord:

Cap-tain, go side - track your train!____

Cap-tain, go side - track your train!____

Num-ber Three in line, A - com-in' in on time,

Cap-tain, go side - track your train.____

Easy as "One, Two..."

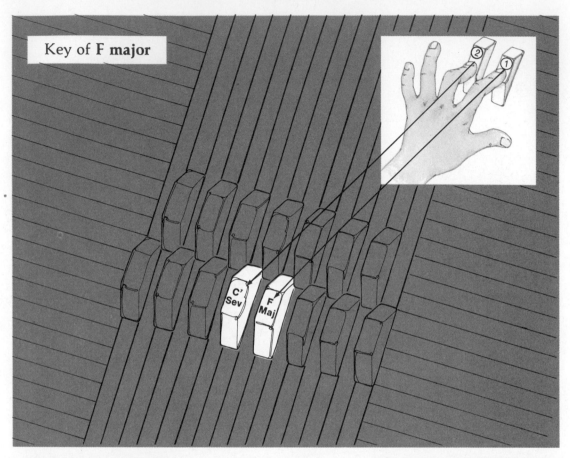

Key of **F major**

CRAWDAD SONG

Start: **2/4**

F
You get a line and I'll get a pole, Honey,

C'
You get a line and I'll get a pole, Babe,

F
You get a line and I'll get a pole,

C'
We'll go down to the crawdad hole,

F   **C'**   **F**
Honey, Babe, mine.

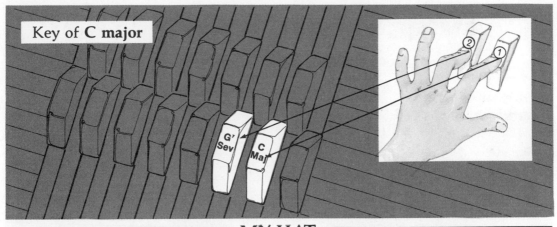

Key of **C major**

MY HAT

Start:  **3/4**

    C   **G'**   **C**

My hat it had three corners, Three corners had my hat;

                G'   **C**

And had it not three corners, It would not be my hat.

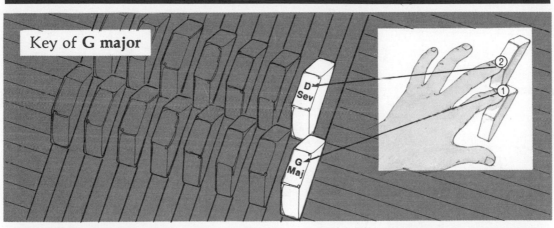

Key of **G major**

THE UPWARD TRAIL

Start:  **4/4**

G   **D'**

We're on the upward trail, we're on the upward trail,

                                 G

Singing, singing, everybody singing, as we go.

                                     D'

We're on the upward trail, we're on the upward trail,

                                 G

Singing, singing, everybody singing, homeward bound.

Easy as "One, Two, Three!"

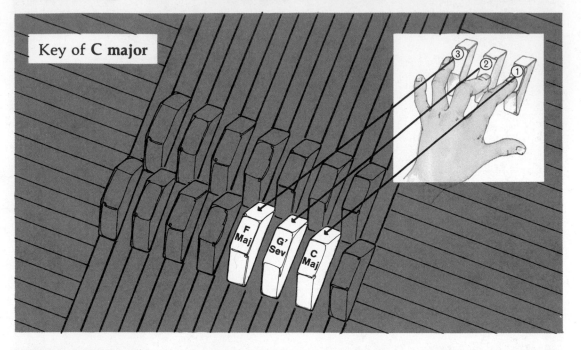

Key of **C major**

MARCHING TO PRETORIA

Start: **E** $\frac{2}{2}$

C
I'm with you and you're with me,
C
And so we are all together,
G⁷
So we are all together,
C
So we are all together.

C
Sing with me, I'll sing with you,
C
And so we will sing together
G⁷   **C**
As we march along.

F   **C**
We are marching to Pretoria,
G⁷   **C**
Pretoria, Pretoria,
F   **C**
We are marching to Pretoria,
G⁷   **C**
Pretoria, hurrah!

- Make up a special introduction and coda on the autoharp.
- How could you use dynamics when performing this song?

154

PLAY SPECIAL ACCOMPANIMENTS

- Play this rhythm pattern as you sing "Mary Ann." Tap the maraca on the autoharp strings as you press down the correct keys.

MARY ANN

Start: (A) 2/2

F   C'
All day, all night, Miss Mary Ann,

                          F
Down by the seaside, sifting sand.

                                    C'
All the little children love Mary Ann,

                          F
You, too, will love her, Miss Mary Ann.

THE CAMPBELLS ARE COMIN'

Scottish Folk Song

- Press down both [D Maj] and [Dm Min] and strum rhythmically.

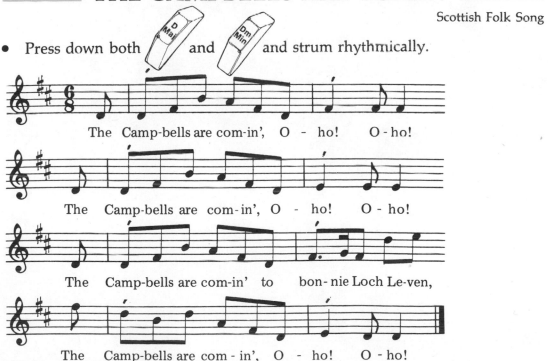

The Camp-bells are com-in', O - ho!   O - ho!

The Camp-bells are com-in', O - ho!   O - ho!

The Camp-bells are com-in' to   bon-nie Loch Le-ven,

The Camp-bells are com-in', O - ho!   O - ho!

155

Be A Describer

THE DESCRIBER

LISTEN ... MOVE ...

DRAW ... TALK ...

DESCRIBE WITH MOVEMENT

JESU, JOY OF MAN'S DESIRING

by Johann Sebastian Bach

Group 1
Move with the steady rhythm of the low strings.

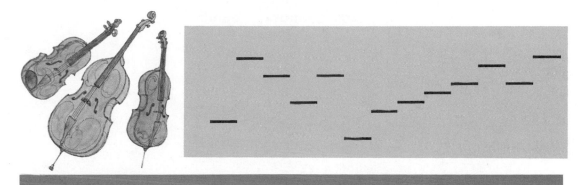

Group 2
Show the constantly moving pattern of the high strings and woodwinds.

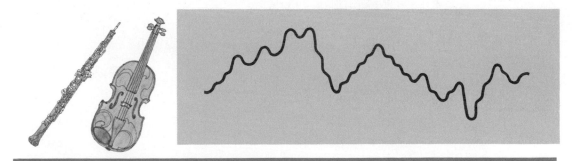

Group 3
Follow the melody of the trumpet.

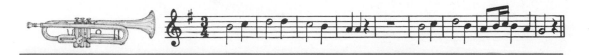

DESCRIBE BY DRAWING

SIX PIECES FOR ORCHESTRA

Third Piece

by Anton Webern

- Can you follow this visual description of the music?
- What did the artist do to describe musical sounds visually?

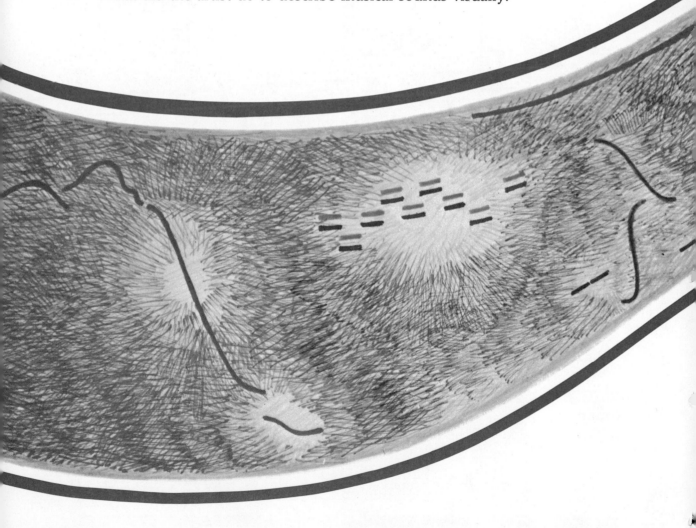

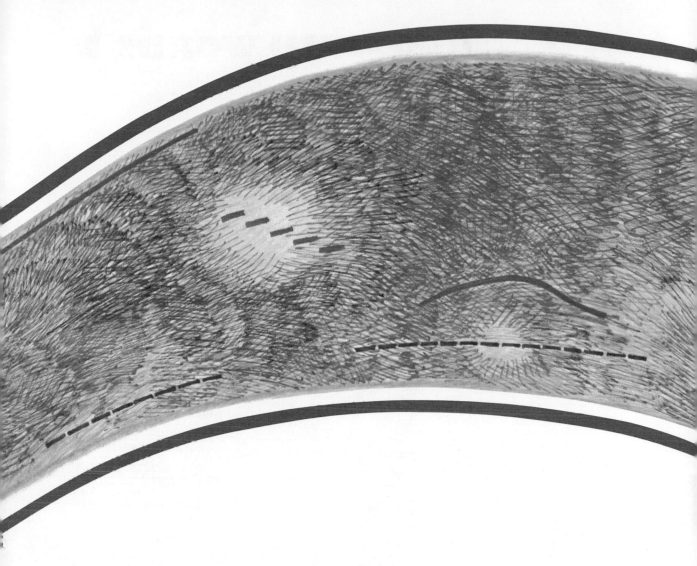

- Listen to another piece by the same composer.

SIX PIECES FOR ORCHESTRA

First Piece

- Can you make your own visual description?

■ DESCRIBE WITH WORDS ■

- Look at "Sun Magic."
  Can you describe . . .
    the **rhythm**?
    the **melody**?
    the **harmony**?
    the **form**?
    the **expression**?

- Listen to "Sun Magic."
  Can you describe . . .
    the **rhythm**?
    the **melody**?
    the **harmony**?
    the **form**?
    the **expression**?

Did your description change after you listened to the song?

SUN MAGIC

Words and Music by Donovan Leitch

1. The sun is a ver - y mag - ic fel - low,
2. The wind is a ver - y fick - le fel - low,
3. The rain is a ver - y sad ___ la - dy,

He shines down on me each day - ay - ay - ay. ___
He blows all my dreams a - way - ay - ay - ay. ___
She falls down on me some - times - ime - ime - imes, ___

The sun is a ver - y mag - ic fel - low,
The wind is a ver - y fick - le fel - low,
The rain is a ver - y sad ___ la - dy,

Bb **C7** **F** **C7**

He shines down on me all day___ ay - ay - ay, ___
Blow - in' all my dreams a - way ___ ay - ay - ay, ___
She falls down on me some - times ___ ime - i - imes, ___

Bb **C7** **F**

He shines down on me each day.___
Blow - in' all my dreams a - way. ___
She falls down on me some - times.___

4. The sea is a very, very old man,
   Deeper than the deepest blue,
   The sea is a very, very old man,
   Deeper than the deepest blue,
   Deeper than the deepest blue.

5. The moon is a typical lady,
   I watch her wax and wane,
   The moon is a typical lady,
   I watch her wax and wane,
   I watch her wax and wane.

6. A star is so very far away, love,
   Just between you and me,
   A star is so very far away, love,
   Just between you and me,
   Just between you and me.

ONE OF THESE IS OUT OF PLACE

Listen to this music.

- You will hear four pieces in each set.
- Three of the pieces are the **same** kind of music.
- One is **different**!
- Can you pick the one that is out of place?

Listen to all the pieces again.

- This time, as you listen, look at the pictures on this page and the next.
- Can you pick the picture that comes from the **same** time and place as the pieces that belong together?

A

B

C

D

E | F

Music of Different Times and Places

What time or place
does this painting
describe?

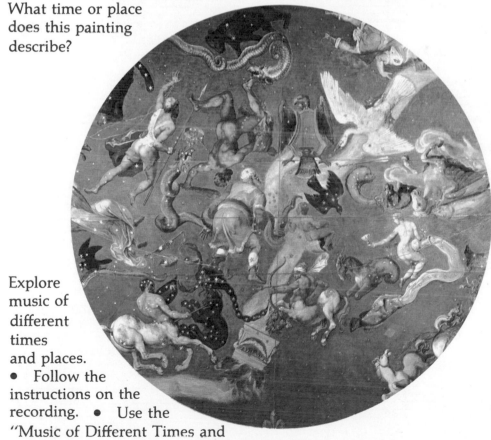

Explore
music of
different
times
and places.
• Follow the
instructions on the
recording. • Use the
"Music of Different Times and
Places" Guide Sheets. • Use instruments to create music of different places.

B: Mural at The University of Morelia. By Alfredo Zalce. C: *Portrait of a Young Man*, c. 1535-40, Bronzino (Agnolo di Cosimo di Mariano; 1503-1572, Italy) Oil on wood, 37⅞″ x 29 ½″. The Metropolitan Museum of Art, New York. Bequest of Mrs. H. O. Havemeyer, 1929. The H. O. Havemeyer Collection. D: Africa: Bambara. Roan antelope headdress representing Tyi wara. From the collection of the American Museum of Natural History, New York. E: Patchwork quilt Ky-Te-3, Index of American Design, National Gallery of Art, Washington, D.C. F: *Little Big Painting*, 1965 Roy Lichtenstein (1923-   , United States) Oil on canvas, 68″ x 80″. Collection of The Whitney Museum of American Art, New York.

163

FACE-DANCE SONG

Transcribed and Arranged
by Louis W. Ballard

As you learn the songs on this page and the following pages,
can you find clues that help you to decide when and where each
song was first sung?

- Look at the words. Can you **see** any clues?
- Listen to the music. Can you **hear** any clues?

Ha - na t'si wah, Ha - na ___ t'si wah, ___

Ha - na ___ t'si wah, Ha - na t'si wah.

Yo - ho wa - ni na - ah yo - ha hey,

Yo - ho wa - ni na yo - ha hey,

Yo - ho wa - ni na - ah yo - ha hey.

164

LABORING SONG

Kwaeja no makashot
(Day dawns with freight to haul)

Rhythmic and spirited

Day dawns with freight to haul, e - ya, e - ya,
Kwae - ja no ma - ka - shot, e - ya, e - ya,

Day dawns with freight to haul, Look for the la - bel!
kwae - ja no ma - ka - shot, ji - ka ma - la - ka!

Day dawns with freight to haul, e - ya, e - ya,
Kwae - ja no ma - ka - shot, e - ya, e - ya,

Day dawns with freight to haul, Look for the la - bel!
kwae - ja no ma - ka - shot, ji - ka ma - la - ka!

THE PURPLE BAMBOO

Add the percussion accompaniment given on the next page.
Someone may make up a recorder part.
Use these pitches: D E F♯ A B

1. See I bring to you pur - ple bam - boo shoot,
2. You must try and grow like the bam - boo tall,

Now 'twill make a love - ly flute;
Then those part - ing lips so small

But those lips so small Can - not play at all
Soon will play the flute Made from bam - boo shoot;

On a love - ly gold - en ___ flute.
Sil - v'ry tunes will gent - ly ___ fall.

Refrain

Ee - tee - tee, Soon will come the hap - py

1.
day.

2.
day. My son the flute will play.

LITTLE FOX

1. Lit - tle fox went out on a chil - ly night;
2. So the fox he ran till he came to the pen;

He prayed to the moon to give him light.
The ducks and the geese were put there - in.

He'd man - y a mile to go that night
"A cou - ple of you will grease my chin

Be - fore he'd reach the town - o, town - o, town - o,
Be - fore I leave this town - o, town - o, town - o,

He'd man - y a mile to go that night
A cou - ple of you will grease my chin

Be - fore he'd reach the town - o.
Be - fore I leave this town - o."

3.   Well he grabbed a grey goose by the neck;
He flung it up across his back.
2 times [He didn't mind the quack, quack, quack,
And the legs all dangling down-o.

4.   Now old Missus Flipperflopper jumped out of bed;
And up to the window she cocked her head.
2 times [She cried, "John, O John, the grey goose is gone,
And the fox is on the town-o."

5.   Little fox he ran till he came to his den;
And there were his little ones, eight, nine, ten.
2 times [They said, "Daddy, you'd better go back again,
It must be a mighty fine town-o."

TROUBADOUR SONG

Words Adapted by William S. Haynie

Music by Colin Muset

Can you describe a troubadour after reading the words?

When cold is the wind, I look for a friend
And there I would stay, no mon - ey to pay,

To give a sing - er a room for the night.
And then be gone with the dawn's ear - ly light.

I'll play on my lute a ron - deau sweet,

If my host will give me food to eat.

Roast pheas - ant and quail, fat duck - ling and hens,

Rich cheese and mut - ton would make us good friends.

Add an accompaniment that sounds like the recording.

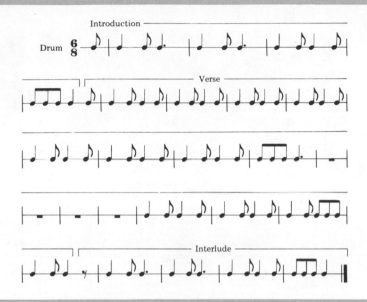

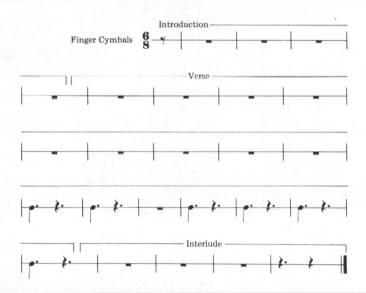

Suggest the sound of the **crumhorn** by playing G on a kazoo.

Suggest the sound of the **lute** by playing chords slowly on the autoharp. Use these chords: When will you change?

THE CROW

Words by Linda Rosenbloom   Music by Igor Stravinsky

On a bridge a-bove the bay Sat a crow one sun-ny day.

I took him by the tail and heel, Then up-on the bridge I__ kneel'd.

In the bay I set him To watch the wa-ter wet him.

Next day I came back to see, Un-der-neath the bridge was he.

I took him out and with a sigh, Put him in the sun to__ dry.

Yes-ter-day I saw him; The sun's still shin-ing on him.

SAN SERENÍ

Spanish Folk Song

Can you sing this song in **thirds**?

- Divide into two groups.
    - **Group 1** sings the top note on each stem.
    - **Group 2** sings the bottom note on each stem.
- Sing the scale numbers for your parts at the same time.
- Listen to the recording. Learn the Spanish words.

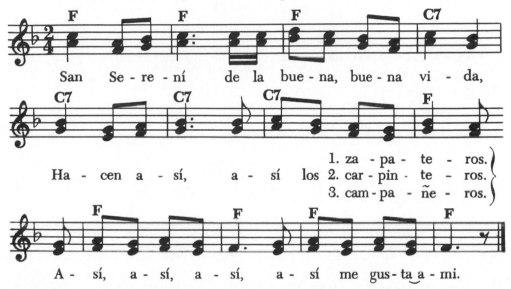

San Se - re - ní de la bue - na, bue - na vi - da,

Ha - cen a - sí, a - sí los
1. za - pa - te - ros.
2. car - pin - te - ros.
3. cam - pa - ñe - ros.

A - sí, a - sí, a - sí, a - sí me gus - ta a - mi.

4. San Serení de la buena, buena vida, Hacen así, así las planchadoras . . .
5. San Serení de la buena, buena vida, Hacen así, así las lavanderas . . .
6. San Serení de la buena, buena vida, Hacen así, así las costureras . . .
7. San Serení de la buena, buena vida, Hacen así, así los jardineros . . .
8. San Serení de la buena, buena vida, Hacen así, así los barquilleros . . .

Add an accompaniment.

- Which instrument will play the shortest sound?

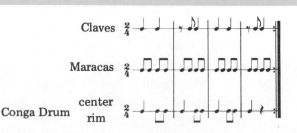

by Jean Dubuffet

BOWERY BUM

Study after Jean Dubuffet
by Ilhan Mimaroglu

Is this music of another time,
                another place,
                now?

What helps you decide?

All the sounds you hear are made
by one "instrument."
• Listen carefully.
• Can you guess what it is?
It is something all of you have used!
It is *not* a real musical instrument.

■ MY MUSIC OF "NOW" ■

Make your own tape-recorder music.
• Find something that makes an interesting sound,
  such as the pencil sharpener.
• Tape record the sound.
    • Play the sound back at a faster speed than it was recorded.
      What happens?
    • Play it at a slower speed.
      What happens now?
• Can you copy your taped sounds onto another tape recorder?
      Make a composition out of them.
• Choose a different "instrument." Tape its sound.
      Can your friends guess what it is?

Dances of Today

THE HOP-SCOTCH POLKA

- Learn the movements for the **A** and **B** sections.
- Repeat the same movements each time the sections are repeated.

Introduction: Get ready to move!

You hop a little on your little left shoe,
You hop a little on your right one, too.
You kick a button like the Scotch kids do,
That's the "Hop-Scotch Polka."

You hop a little on your little left shoe,
You hop a little on your right one, too.
You don't mind bouncin' like a kangaroo
To the "Hop-Scotch Polka."

It's in and out among the maple trees.
It's up and down and then you wave your knees.
You head goes bobbin' in the morning breeze
To the "Hop-Scotch Polka."

You hop a little on your little left shoe,
You hop a little on your right one, too.
You kick a button like the Scotch kids do,
That's the "Hop-Scotch Polka."

Complete the dance in the following manner:

B A A Coda

Dance of Another Land

TINIKLING

Philippine Folk Dance

PLAYERS

Two players sit on the floor and hold the ends of bamboo poles.

Introduction:

- Begin when the music begins.
- Slide poles together on beat 1.
- Lift the poles apart and tap the wood on beats 2 and 3.

Section A:

- Continue playing the "pole rhythm."

click tap tap click tap tap

Section B:

- Continue as before.

DANCERS

Two dancers face each other from across the poles.

Introduction:

- Listen for 4 measures. Then tap right toes between the poles on beats 2 and 3 for 4 measures.

rest tap tap rest tap tap

rest tap tap rest tap tap

Section A:

Beat 1 ♩ Hop on left foot outside of poles.

Beat 2 ♩ Step between poles with right foot.

Beat 3 ♩ Step between poles with left foot.

Measure 2: Repeat, starting with *right* foot.

Section B:

- Walk outside the poles: left foot, right foot, left foot, right foot.
- Leap inside the poles: right foot, left foot.
- Repeat, starting with *right* foot.

Dances of Another Land

LA RASPA

Mexican Folk Dance

How well can you follow dance instructions?
Learn the movements for this Mexican dance.

A-section of the music

Dance in partners

Step I
L-hop; right heel out

Step II
R-hop; left heel out

B-section of the music

Take eight running steps clockwise.
Release partners, clap hands.
Repeat steps, moving counter-clockwise.

Find a partner.
Perform the entire dance.
You will hear the **A-section** five times
and the **B-section** five times.

Swing your partner

Play-Party Time

YOUR BEST LIKING

1. Meeting halfway with your best liking,
   Meeting halfway with your best liking,
   Meeting halfway with your best liking,
   For she is your darling.
2. Right hand round, etc.
3. Left hand round, etc.
4. Both hands round, etc.
5. Do-si-do, etc.
6. Turn right and left, etc.
7. All run away, etc.

SKIP TO MY LOU

1. Gents to the center, Skip to my Lou;
   Gents to the center, Skip to my Lou;
   Gents to the center, Skip to my Lou;
   Skip to my Lou, my darling!
2. Ladies to the center, etc.
3. Bow to your partner, etc.
4. Now to your opposite, etc.
5. Promenade all and, etc.
6. Lost my lover, what shall I do?
7. I found another one, just as true.

Dances of Another Time

TWO DUCTIAE

Anonymous

Listen to music of long ago.
Then learn to dance as the knights and ladies did.
FORMATION: A double circle of partners.
INTRODUCTION: Face your partner; bow or curtsey:

$\frac{3}{8}$ 𝅗𝅥. | 𝅗𝅥. | 𝅗𝅥. | 𝅗𝅥. |

      step back   bend knees   straighten knees   feet together

DANCE: Join right hands. Step around the circle.

Double forward: $\frac{3}{8}$ 𝅗𝅥. | 𝅗𝅥. | 𝅗𝅥. | 𝅗𝅥. |

    left foot forward   right foot forward   left foot forward   right foot together

Double backward: $\frac{3}{8}$ 𝅗𝅥. | 𝅗𝅥. | 𝅗𝅥. | 𝅗𝅥. |

    right foot back   left foot back   right foot back   left foot together

Simple left: $\frac{3}{8}$ 𝅗𝅥. | 𝅗𝅥. |

    left foot steps sideways   right foot steps together

Simple right: $\frac{3}{8}$ 𝅗𝅥. | 𝅗𝅥. |

    right foot steps sideways   left foot steps together

- Repeat your steps over and over.
- Can you dance in a stately style like the people of long ago?

BE A COMPOSER

THE COMPOSER

ARRANGE . . . IMPROVISE . . .
COMPOSE . . . CREATE . . .

BICYCLE BOURRÉE

- Play the numbered positions on the bicycle.
- Use the mallet indicated.
- You decide how long to perform each part of the score before moving on.

Sound Starters

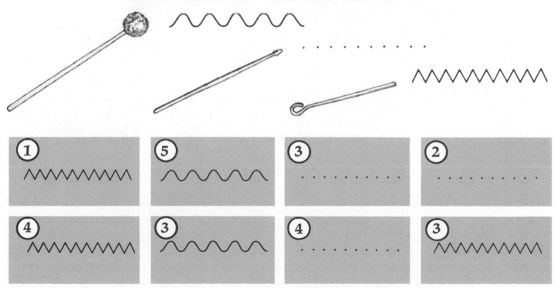

- Create your own score. Can you find other **timbres** on the bicycle?

MAKE YOUR OWN INSTRUMENT

- Use or adapt the ideas on the following pages
        or
- Make up your own ideas.

THERE IS ONLY ONE RULE!

You must be able to play at least **two different pitches** on your instrument.

Wooden and plastic bowls
floating in water

Two-tone
nail piano

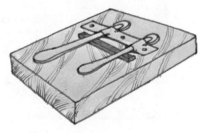

Suspended garbage-can
lids (different sizes),
spikes, bottles, metal
tubes

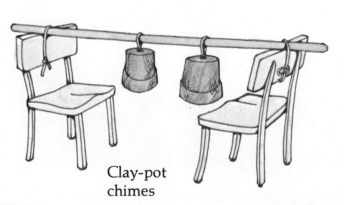

Clay-pot
chimes

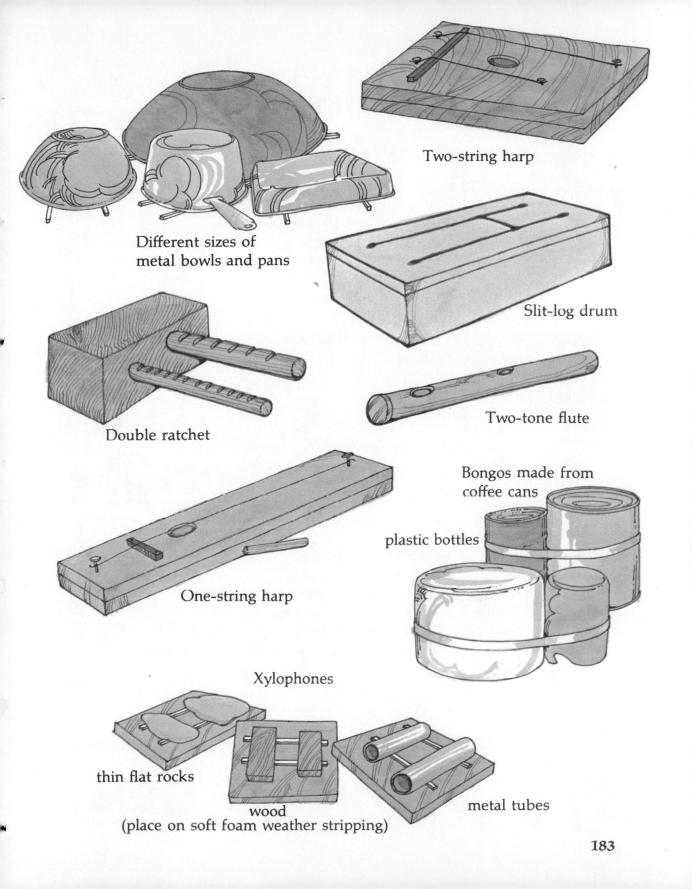

Two-string harp

Different sizes of
metal bowls and pans

Slit-log drum

Double ratchet

Two-tone flute

One-string harp

Bongos made from
coffee cans

plastic bottles

Xylophones

thin flat rocks

wood
(place on soft foam weather stripping)

metal tubes

183

Use Your Instruments

Work in small groups. Create a chance composition.

- Stand side by side in a row. Take turns playing the two pitches on each instrument to create a "tone row."
- Can you make a "melody" out of this row?
  To make your melody, you may repeat pitches, use longer and shorter sounds, or sometimes not play at all.
- How do the different **timbres** add interest to your piece?
- What happens when people change places in the row?

Use Your Instruments

Work in small groups. Create a piece using **harmony**.

- Choose one or more instruments to play an **ostinato** pattern.
- Use other instruments with the **ostinato.**
  When should certain **timbres** of instruments be heard?
  Will you use one or both **pitches** on your instrument?
  Will you repeat any of your patterns?
  How can you use expressive ideas such as **dynamics, tempo, articulation**?
- Select one person to **conduct** the group.
- Perform the piece for others in the class.

Use Your Instruments

Perform as a large ensemble.

- Group together instruments of similar **pitch** and **timbre.**
- Select a **conductor/composer.**
- Decide what signals the **conductor** should use to tell the group which sounds to perform.

A specific performer should play.

Stop playing.

Play louder.

Everyone should play.

Play softer.

What other signals will you need?

- Perform the piece.
  How do you like your piece?
- What in the music made you feel the way you do about the piece?
- What would you suggest to a **conductor** to improve or change the music?

A TIMELY RHYME

Words Anonymous   Music by Jean Moe

Play these three **scales.**
Which ones do you know?
Can you find melody patterns based on each **scale**?

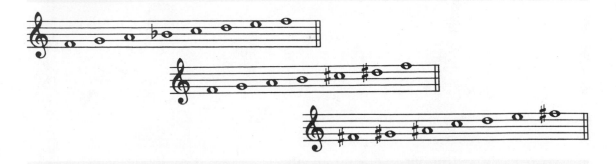

The time of day I do not tell as some do by the clock,

Or by the dis - tant chim - ing bell set on some stee - pled rock;

But by the pro - gress that I see in what I have to do,

It's ei - ther "done o' - clock" for me, or on - ly "half - past through."

186

It's Time

- Play this tune three ways.
- Use the bells for each **scale** shown on page 186.

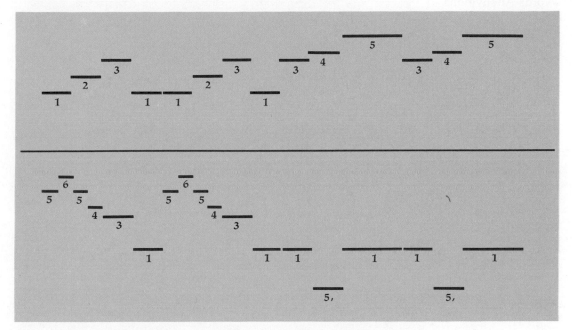

What happened to the song when you played it using one of the new **whole-tone scales**?

- Compose a melody for this rhyme.
  Use six pitches: 1 2 3 4 5 6
- Perform it using a **major scale** and then a **whole-tone scale.** Can you play it in **minor**? Which **steps** will you need to change?

UNSQUARE DANCE

by Dave Brubeck

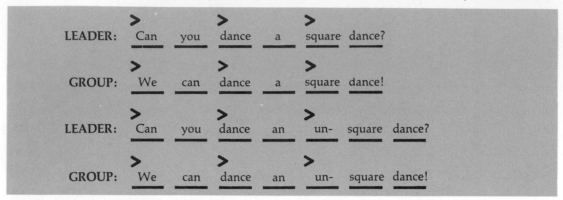

	>		>		>	
LEADER:	Can	you	dance	a	square	dance?

	>		>		>	
GROUP:	We	can	dance	a	square	dance!

	>		>		>		
LEADER:	Can	you	dance	an	un-	square	dance?

	>		>		>		
GROUP:	We	can	dance	an	un-	square	dance!

Listen to an unsquare dance.
Why is this a good title for this music?
Listen for these patterns.
Can you tap them?
Tap only on the accents.

>		>		>		
Fid-	dle,	fid-	dle,	bass	fid-	dle.

	>		>		>	>
Hand	clap,	hand	clap,	hand	clap-	ping.

Your Unsquare Dance

Plan your own unsquare dance. Work in pairs.
Use percussion instruments. Chant the name of each instrument.

Then tap each syllable on the instrument.
Accent the first syllable.
Decide on an order for chanting the names.

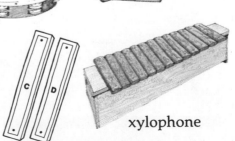

• Add a melody on bells

xylophone

STEPPING-A-ROUND

Get ready!

* Copy this design on a large piece of wrapping paper and put it on the floor. The small boxes in the outer circle should be about the length of your foot.

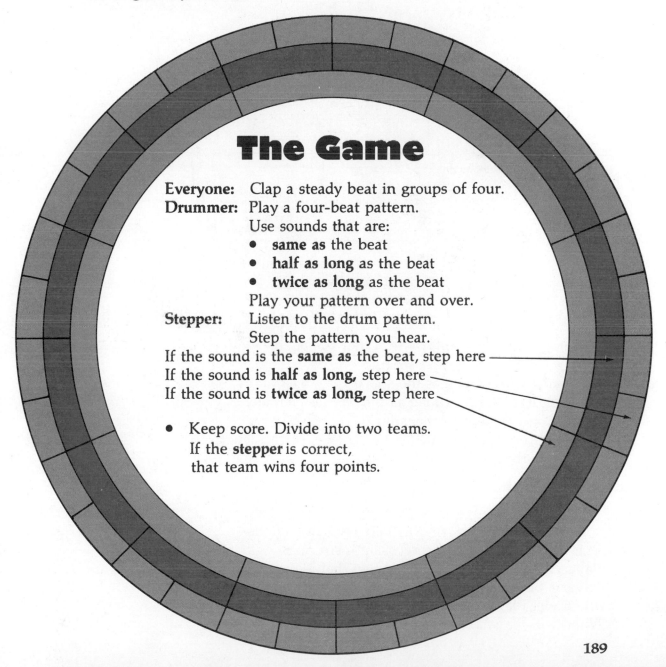

The Game

Everyone: Clap a steady beat in groups of four.
Drummer: Play a four-beat pattern.
Use sounds that are:
* **same as** the beat
* **half as long** as the beat
* **twice as long** as the beat

Play your pattern over and over.

Stepper: Listen to the drum pattern.
Step the pattern you hear.

If the sound is the **same as** the beat, step here
If the sound is **half as long,** step here
If the sound is **twice as long,** step here

* Keep score. Divide into two teams.
If the **stepper** is correct,
that team wins four points.

▰ PERCUSSION-A-ROUND ▰

Get ready!

- Draw two circles on a large piece of wrapping paper.

- Divide the inner circle into sixteen equal beats. Number them.

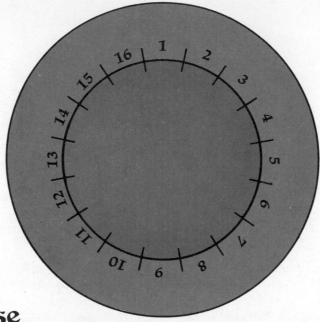

Compose

Make up a sixteen-count rhythm that sometimes moves
- **with** the shortest sound
- **twice as long** as the shortest sound
- **four times as long** as the shortest sound

Could you use other relationships?

Divide the outer circle into "boxes" of the correct length to show your rhythm. Draw them in.

Perform

Four people may perform this Percussion-a-Round.

Each chooses a different percussion instrument.

Player 1 begins with count 1. When that player reaches 5,
Player 2 begins.

When will **Player 3** begin?

When will **Player 4** begin?

RUFFORD PARK POACHERS

from Lincolnshire Posy
by Percy Grainger

In early England, the King kept a park especially for his own hunting pleasure. But other hunters sometimes would steal into the park to poach the King's deer. Listen as the music describes three poachers . . .

SECTION A

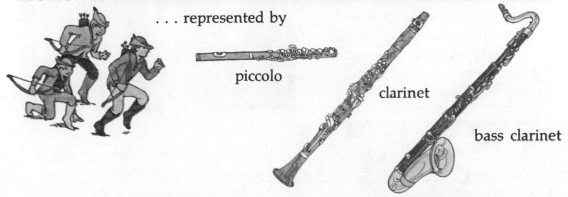

. . . represented by

piccolo

clarinet

bass clarinet

. . . trailing one another in a **canon.**

SECTION B

- The orchestra plays a syncopated accompaniment to the trumpet's melody. Other brass instruments warn of danger.
- Waves of loud crescendos and a minor tonality portray the shadowy movement of the poachers. Rapid fluttering sounds add to the feeling of a dangerous deed.
- A musical peak is reached. The poachers seem to retreat.

SECTION A

The low brass drones on as the poachers retrace their trail and sneak away. The **canon** is heard again.

- Do you think the poachers really took anything?

191

MUSICIANS AT WORK IN A MUSIC STORE

If you worked in a music store, which career would you like?

If you worked in the **Instrument Department,** you would need to:
- know the features of each instrument.
- know something about how various instruments are played.
- be able to recommend suitable instruments for people of all ages and abilities.

If you worked in a **Sheet Music Department,** you would need to:
- organize your stock so that titles can be located quickly.
- recommend music for beginners on each instrument.
- know which selections are available for various instrumental and choral groups.

If you worked in a **Record Department,** you would need to:
- know how to locate requested titles in your stock and in the catalogs.
- operate tape decks and record players.
- keep up to date on the latest records released.

If you worked as the **Studio Teacher,** you would need to:
- give instrumental or voice lessons to individuals or groups.
- organize student recitals.
- coach small instrumental ensembles.

If you worked in the **Instrument Repair Department,** you would need to:
- repair, clean, and replace parts on all instruments and check them by playing.
- fit new instruments with the proper parts or accessories.
- tune pianos.

If you worked in the **Electronic Equipment Department,** you would need to:
- know about the quality and special features of different types of recording and playback equipment.
- be able to demonstrate electric instruments—guitars, pianos, and others.
- know about amplifiers and microphones.

Turn your classroom into a **music store.** Which of these jobs can you become qualified to do?

A NEW WAY TO SING ROUNDS

Learn these two rounds.
Divide into two groups. Sing the two rounds at the same time.
Which group will need to sing its song twice?

WHY SHOULDN'T MY GOOSE?

Traditional Round

Why should-n't my goose Grow as fat as thy goose,

When I paid for my goose Twice as much as thine?

CHERRIES SO RIPE

Traditional Round

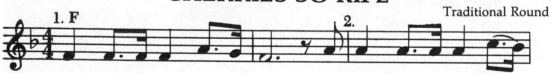

Cher - ries so ripe and so round, The best in the mar-ket _

found, On - ly a pen - ny a pound. Who will buy?

Try singing "De Bezem," page 36, and "Row, Row, Row Your Boat"
at the same time. Begin both songs on C.

■ COMPOSE-A-ROUND ■

- Make up a two-phrase chant.
  Use these nonsense words or make up your own.

ZIGGLE WIGGLE

TRAK

TRIK   TROK

KATABLOOM

ROSADOOM   PHTT

- Tap beats in groups of four.
- Say your chant over and over while you tap.
- When you have a rhythm, add a melody.
  Use any of these pitches:

- Play your song.
- Sing it.
- Teach it to a friend.
- Perform it as a round.

Can you sing your melody while someone else sings
"Why Shouldn't My Goose" or "Cherries So Ripe"?

THEME & VARIATIONS ON A HANDSHAKE

Greet your friend. Shake hands. Try variations on handshakes.

THEME　　　　**VARIATION 1**　　　　**VARIATION 2**

Create a "Theme and Variation on a Handshake for Sixteen Dancers."

INTRODUCTION:	Two people walk toward each other.
THEME:	Greet each other, shaking hands in the usual way.
INTERLUDE:	These two people walk to greet two new people.
VARIATION 1:	These four people shake hands.
	Use the first variation.
INTERLUDE:	These four people greet four new people.
VARIATION 2:	These eight people shake hands.
	Use the second variation.

Perform two more variations. Insert the interlude between each.

Can you think of other ways to shake hands?
Can you change the **rhythm** of your handshakes? the **tempo**?

by Georges Bizet

Allegro

Andante

Staccato

Marcato

- Sing the song on page 212.
  It is the theme for this composition.
- Follow the notation of the song as
  you listen to the "Prelude."
- Next, listen to four **variations**
  on the **theme.**
- Is anything the same each time?
- What has been changed?
- Talk about the changes you hear.
  Use musical terms you have learned.

Legato

Major

Minor

Unison

Harmony

Melody

Rhythm

Forte

Phrase

Piano

Ritardando

Crescendo

Decrescendo

Accelerando

Accompaniment

H.M.S. PINAFORE

Words by Sir William Gilbert

Music by Sir Arthur Sullivan

We sail the ocean blue, and our saucy ship's a beauty;
We're sober men and true, and attentive to our duty.
When the balls whistle free o'er the bright blue sea,
We stand to our guns all day;
When at anchor we ride on the Portsmouth tide,
We've plenty of time for play.
A-hoy! A-hoy! The balls whistle free;
A-hoy! A-hoy! O'er the bright blue sea,
We stand to our guns, to our guns all day.
We sail the ocean blue and our saucy ship's a beauty,
We're sober men and true and attentive to our duty;
Our saucy ship's a beauty, we're attentive to our duty;
We're sober men and true, we sail the ocean blue.

I'm called Little Buttercup,
Dear Little Buttercup,
Though I could never tell why,
But still I'm called Buttercup,
Poor Little Buttercup,
Sweet Little Buttercup I!

CAPTAIN: I am the captain of the Pinafore!
CREW: And a right good captain, too!
CAPTAIN: You're very, very good,
     and, be it understood,
       I command a right good crew.
CREW: We're very, very good,
     and, be it understood,
       He commands a right good crew.
CAPTAIN: Though related to a peer,
     I can hand, reef and steer, Or ship a selvagee;
     I am never known to quail at the fury of a gale,
     And I'm never, never sick at sea!
CREW: What, never?
CAPTAIN: No, never!
CREW: What, never?
CAPTAIN: Well, hardly ever!
CREW: He's hardly ever sick at sea!
     Then give three cheers, and one cheer more,
     For the hardy captain of the Pinafore!
     Then give three cheers, and one cheer more,
     For the captain of the Pinafore!

SAILORS: Carefully on tiptoe stealing,
        Breathing gently as we may,
        Every step with caution feeling,
        We will softly steal away.
        Goodness me! Why, what was that?
DEADEYE: Silent be, it was the cat!
SAILORS: It was, it was the cat!
CAPTAIN: They're right, it was the cat!
SAILORS: Pull ashore in fashion steady,
        My men will defray the fare,
        For a clergy man is ready to unite the happy pair!
        Goodness me, why, what was that?
DEADEYE: Silent be, again that cat!
SAILORS: It was again that cat!
CAPTAIN: They're right, it was the cat!
ALL: Every step with caution feeling,
    We will softly steal away,
    Every step with caution feeling,
    We will softly steal away.

CREATE YOUR OWN DRAMA

SCENE: An automobile assembly plant
CHARACTERS: Worker   Owner
                  Supervisor Designer

- Which one will you play?
- Will you be: young? old? . . . tall? short? . . . happy? grouchy? . . . tired? lively? . . .
- What will you do?
- What will you say to each other?

ACTION: an ordinary day at the plant . . .
Suddenly! one worker notices that a kitten has somehow got into the building. It is walking on a narrow ledge over the turning, grinding machinery of the assembly line!
ACTION: (Complete the drama.)

Discuss your performance. Are there any changes you want to make?

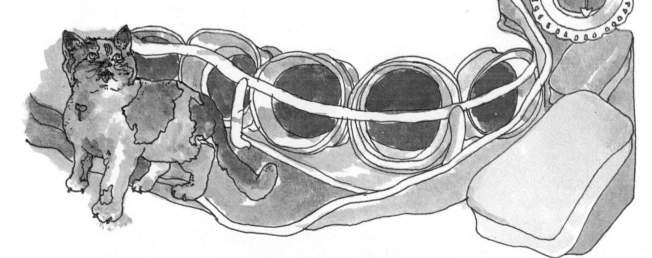

Create Your Own Opera

Perform this drama again. This time, sing all the speaking parts.
Create your own opera!

CAPTAIN HOOK AND THE CROCODILE

Adapted from the play by James Barrie

Music by B.A.

Captain Hook was a wicked pirate. He walked on his peg leg with
a swagger and a loud thump!

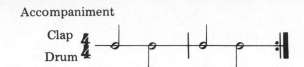

Accompaniment

Clap

Drum

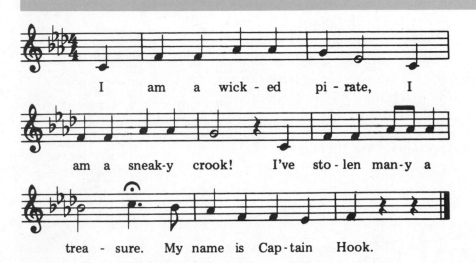

I am a wick - ed pi - rate, I

am a sneak-y crook! I've sto - len man-y a

trea - sure. My name is Cap - tain Hook.

Only one sound could frighten Captain Hook. That was the sound
of a "Tick! Tock!" that came from the inside of a special
crocodile. This crocodile had once tasted the Captain's hand
and foot. At the same time, the crocodile had swallowed a very
loud ticking clock!
The crocodile was hungry for more, but the Captain always heard
the warning of the "Tick! Tock!" when the crocodile was near.

Wood Block

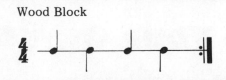

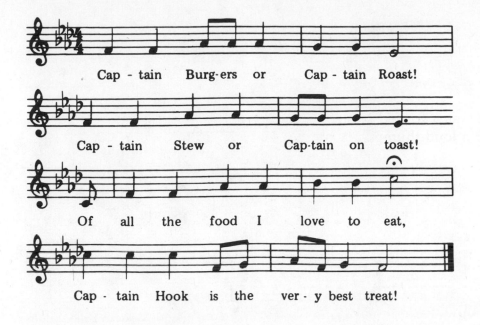

Cap - tain Burg-ers or Cap - tain Roast!

Cap - tain Stew or Cap-tain on toast!

Of all the food I love to eat,

Cap - tain Hook is the ver - y best treat!

After trying many times, the crocodile finally found Captain Hook. This is what happened:

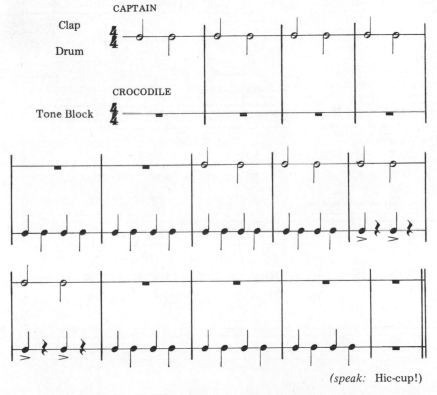

CAPTAIN

Clap

Drum

CROCODILE

Tone Block

(speak: Hic-cup!)

- Why are the instruments important to this drama?

Music for Special Times

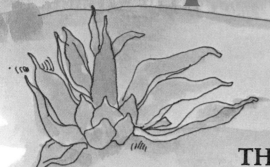

THE MORNING
(LAS MAÑANITAS)

English Words Adapted

Mexican Folk Melody

How beau-ti-ful is the morn-ing;____
Qué lin-da es-tá la ma-ña-na,____

It's a ver-y____ spe-cial day.____
en que ven-go a____ sa-lu-dar-te,____

The sun in the east is dawn-ing,____
Ve-ni-mos to-dos reu-ni-dos,____

And we've come to you to say:____
con pla-cer a fe-li-ci-tar-te,____ Ya

Hap - py birth - day, my good {boy, {girl,
vie - ne a - ma - ne - cien - do, ya

Get up! Your birth - day's here. _____
la luz del día nos di - o; _____

May the joys of peace and friend - ship ___
A - le - ván - ta - te, a - mi - gui - to, ___

Bring a ver - y spe - cial year! _____
¡mi - ra que ya a - ma - ne - ció! _____

205

A TERRIFYING SIGHT!

Adapted by B. Andress

Perform this ghost story. Speak the parts of the **Narrator** and **Peasant**.

Sing the **Ghost's** words with three pitches:

Narrator: A poor peasant and his donkey
Came upon a castle one night.
They were warned it was haunted.
By a Ghost . . . a frightful sight!

When they were inside
They heard a door creak open.
Something moaned and groaned.
As these words were spoken:

Ghost: My legs I've lost,
Oh, woe is me.
Rubies to him
Who finds them for me.

Narrator: And with that, two legs fell
Straight through the door
And hit with a thump
On the old castle floor.

Peasant: Here! Here! My good Ghost,
You can't frighten me
By flip-flopping your legs
For me to see!

Ghost: My arms I've lost,
Oh, woe is me.
Diamonds to him
Who finds them for me.

Narrator: And with that, two arms fell
Straight through the door
And hit with a thump
On the old castle floor.

Peasant: Here! Here! My good Ghost,
You can't frighten me
By flip-flopping your arms
For me to see!

Ghost: My head I've lost,
Oh, woe is me.
Gold to him
Who finds it for me.

Narrator: And with that, a head fell
Straight through the door
And landed on the hand
That had fallen just before.

Peasant: Well, I must admit,
For a Ghost you're a mess
Come on, little donkey,
We'll help him, I guess!

Narrator: So they pushed and they pulled
And sorted the parts,
And finally made him look
Like he did at the start!

(Ghost moves out from behind desk.)

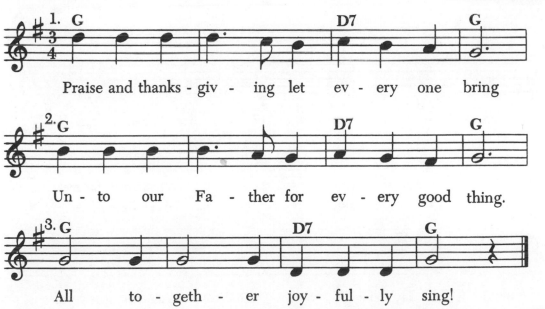

PRAISE AND THANKSGIVING

Traditional Round

Praise and thanks-giv-ing let ev-ery one bring

Un-to our Fa-ther for ev-ery good thing.

All to-geth-er joy-ful-ly sing!

207

O HANUKAH

Translated by Judith Eisenstein

Yiddish Folk Song

O Ha - nu - kah, O Ha - nu - kah, come light the me - no - rah,

Let's have a par - ty, we'll all dance the ho - ra.

Gath - er round the ta - ble, we'll give you a treat,

Shin - ing tops to play with and pan - cakes to eat;

And while we are play - ing the can - dles are burn - ing_ low.

One for each night, they_ shed a sweet light To re -

mind us of days long a - go.   mind us of days long a - go.

WE WISH YOU A MERRY CHRISTMAS

English Folk Song

We wish you a mer-ry Christ-mas, we wish you a mer-ry Christ-mas,

Fine

We wish you a mer-ry Christ-mas and a hap-py New Year.

Good tid - ings we bring for you and your kin:

Good tid - ings of Christ - mas and a hap - py New Year.

1. Now bring us some fig - gy pud - ding, now
2. We won't go un - til we get some, we

bring us some fig - gy pud - ding, Now
won't go un - til we get some, We

(after verse 2, D.C. al Fine)

bring us some fig - gy pud - ding, and bring some right here.
won't go un - til we get some, so bring some right here.

CHRISTMAS IS COMING

Traditional English Round

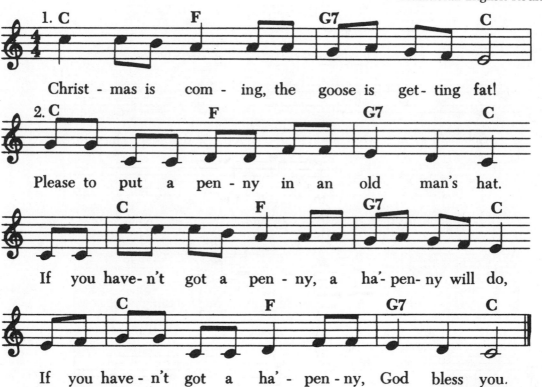

1. Christ - mas is com - ing, the goose is get - ting fat!

2. Please to put a pen - ny in an old man's hat.

If you have - n't got a pen - ny, a ha' - pen - ny will do,

If you have - n't got a ha' - pen - ny, God bless you.

- Can you plan a dance for this song?
- Perhaps you can use some of these movements.
  Join hands in a circle. Move to left or right.
  Drop hands, walk to the center.
  Walk backwards, to place.
- What will you do on the words "put a penny"?

210

ARRURU

English Words by Elena Paz

Spanish Folk Melody

1. Se - ño - ra do - ña Ma - rí - a,
2. The shep - herds are slow - ly wind - ing
3. A - blaze in the win - try sky, _____

I bring you my lit - tle one.
Their way from the dis - tant hills,
The dia - mond of Beth - le - hem,

He'll help you to rock the cra - dle,
To wit - ness the new - born Ba - by,
How bright is the star on high, _____

Where - in lies your new - born son.
They've braved all of win - ter's ills.
O - ver Je - ru - sa - lem.

Refrain

A - rru - ru, a - rru - ru,

Duer - me - te, Ni - ño Je - sús. sús.

MARCH OF THE KINGS

Translated by Satis Coleman

French Folk Melody

Three great kings _ I met at ear - ly morn, _ With all their
Ce ma - tin, _ J'ai ren - con - tré le train _ De trois grands

ret - i - nue were slow - ly march - ing; Three great
Rois qui al - laient en voy - a - ge, Ce ma -

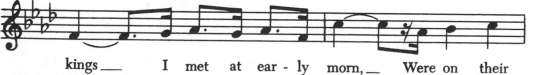

kings _ I met at ear - ly morn, _ Were on their
tin, _ J'ai ren - con - tré le train _ De trois grands

way to meet the new - ly born. With gifts of
Rois des - sus le grand che - min. Tout char - gés

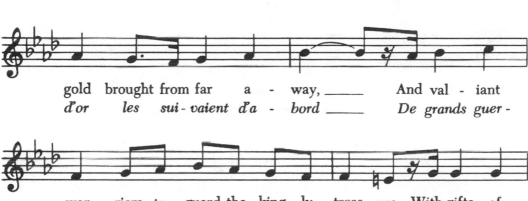

gold brought from far a - way, _____ And val - iant
d'or les sui - vaient d'a - bord _____ De grands guer -

war - riors to guard the king - ly treas - ure, With gifts of
riers et les gar - des du tré - sor, _____ Tout char - gés

gold brought from far a - way, _____ And shields all
d'or les sui - vaient d'a - bord _____ De grands guer -

shin - ing in their bright ar - ray.
riers a - vec leurs bou - cli - ers.

LO, THE WINTER IS PAST

Words from the "Song of Solomon"   Music by Walter Ihrke

Very smoothly

For, lo,   the win - ter is past;   the rain is __

o - ver and gone.   The flow - ers ap - pear on the earth; the

time of the sing - ing of birds is come. __

214

IT IS PURIM, BROTHERS

Words adapted

Music by A. Goldfaden

It is Pu-rim, broth-ers, Best hol - i-day of all.

Sis-ters, let us sing now, At ev-ery house we'll call.

Mor-de-cai be gay, Be mer-ry and play, We re - live this

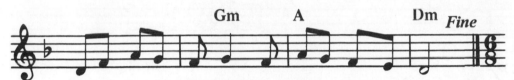

day ev-ery   year.___ Come sing, chil-dren, sing! Come

dance, have your fling! Re-mem-ber this day, oh so dear.___

THE STAR-SPANGLED BANNER

Words by Francis Scott Key

Composer Unknown

1. Oh,— say, can you see   by the dawn's ear - ly light,
2. On the shore, dim - ly seen   thro' the mists of the deep,
3. Oh, — thus be it ev-er when — free men shall stand

What so proud - ly we   hailed at the twi - light's last gleam-ing?
Where the foe's haugh-ty   host   in dread si - lence re - pos - es,
Be - tween their loved homes and the war's des - o - la - tion!

Whose broad stripes and bright stars, through the per - il - ous fight,
What is that which the breeze, o'er the tow - er - ing steep,
Blest with vic - t'ry and peace, may the heav'n-res - cued land

O'er the ram - parts we watched were so gal - lant - ly stream-ing?
As it fit - ful - ly blows, half con - ceals, half dis - clos - es?
Praise the Pow'r that hath made and pre - served us a   na - tion.

And the rock - ets' red glare, the bombs burst- ing in   air,
Now it catch - es the gleam of the morn- ing's first beam,
Then — con - quer we must, for our cause it is just,

216

CLASSIFIED INDEX

ALPHABETICAL INDEX